# THE PROMISE
# OF POWER

LIFE MESSAGES OF
GREAT CHRISTIANS

# The Promise of Power

JAMIE BUCKINGHAM

Compiled by
JUDITH COUCHMAN

SERVANT PUBLICATIONS
ANN ARBOR, MICHIGAN

Vine Books is an imprint of Servant Publications especially designed to serve
evangelical Christians.

Unless otherwise noted, the Scripture used is from the King James version of the
Bible. All other verses are from the macBible © 1987, 1988, 1991, 1993 by
Zondervan Corporation. Verses marked NRSV are taken from the New Revised
Standard Version of the Bible © 1989 by the Division of Christian Education of the
National Council of Churches of Christ in the United States of America, and used by
permission. All rights reserved. Verses marked NIV are from the Holy Bible, New
International Version © 1973, 1978, 1984 by The International Bible Society. All
rights reserved. Macintosh is a trademark of Apple Computer, Inc.

*The Promise of Power* is compiled from the following works of Jamie Buckingham: *A
Way Through the Wilderness; Bible People Like Me; Risky Living;* and *Where Eagles
Soar.* These excerpts are published by special arrangement with and permission of
Jackie Buckingham. All rights reserved.

Published by Servant Publications
P.O. Box 8617
Ann Arbor, Michigan 48107

Cover design: Hile Illustration and Design, Ann Arbor, MI

98 99 00  10 9 8 7 6 5 4 3 2 1
Printed in the United States of America
ISBN 1-56955-079-4

LIBRARY OF CONGRESS CATALOGING-IN-PUBLICATION DATA

Buckingham, Jamie.
    The promise of power / Jamie Buckingham ; compiled by Judith Couchman.
        p.    cm. — (Life messages of great Christians)
    Includes bibliographical references.
    ISBN 1-56955-079-4 (alk paper)
    1. Devotional calendars.    2. Spiritual life—Christianity—Meditations.
I. Couchman, Judith, 1953-    .  II. Title.  III. Series.
BV4811.B823    1998
242—dc21                                        98-34359
                                                CIP

*For The Vision Group,*
*a collection of powerful, promising women*

# Contents

# Acknowledgments

~

I AM GRATEFUL FOR the editorial team at Servant Publications who worked with me on this devotional: Bert Ghezzi, Liz Heaney, Heidi Hess and Deena Davis. To be sure, they are competent experts, but I also appreciate them as wonderful friends.

Charette Barta, Opal Couchman, Win Couchman, Madalene Harris, Karen Hilt, Shirley Honeywell, Mae Lammers and Nancy Lemons also deserve many thanks for their prayers as I worked on this book. May their prayers be multiplied into the lives of its readers.

There are also many friends who support my work, but I especially want to thank Janel Ferguson, who for several years has listened, encouraged and applauded me through projects I've written or compiled. Thank you, Janel, for your enduring friendship and support.

Most of all, I'm indebted to Jackie Buckingham for allowing me to excerpt from her husband's out-of-print books, keeping alive his memory and ministry. I thank her, and so do many of Jamie's longtime and newfound readers.

# Introduction

~

I FIRST MET JAMIE BUCKINGHAM about fifteen years ago in the pages of his book, *The Last Word.* I was house-sitting for some friends, and out of boredom I picked up the hardback and read a few here-and-there entries. It didn't take long to get hooked, and I remember reclining in bed late that night, still reading, so I could finish the book before my friends returned from their weekend getaway.

I'm sure these friends would have loaned the book to me, but that wasn't the point. Jamie grabbed my attention and didn't let go. His straightforwardness forced me to consider my walk with God, and his honesty assured me of his imperfections and empathy for my own shortcomings. And, of course, there was the humor. When Jamie turned the spotlight on his own character flaws and failings, he laughed at himself, as if to say, "Take God seriously, but don't take *yourself* seriously."

Without a doubt, Jamie took God seriously. He longed for all that God offers and pursued his spiritual purpose with passion. "Our loving God has created each one of us to do best that which we enjoy doing," wrote Jamie. "A number of years ago, I determined the best way to make this principle effective

11

in my own life was to find the one thing I enjoy doing more than any other, then figure out a way to get people to pay me for doing it. In my case, that is what I am doing now—writing a book. In your case, it may be something else. Whatever it is, the Potter has designed something into each one of us which needs to be sanctified, some special gift which when discovered and put into use, will bring you happiness and satisfaction by fulfilling the desire of your heart."[1]

Jamie also believed that following God's purpose meant the promise of spiritual power. "Are miracles for today?" he asked, and answered, "Only if Jesus is for today. For He has not changed—and His Spirit in us is still the same miracle-working Spirit as when He descended upon Jesus at the Jordan River. By giving us the same Spirit He received at His baptism, He indwells us and empowers us and in and through and by us presents Himself to every generation and every place."[2]

True to this belief, Jamie took the gospel's message of purpose and power to his generation. After serving as a pastor he decided to pursue "the thing he enjoyed," writing more than forty books, including those he coauthored with notables such as Nicky Cruz, Kathryn Kuhlman, Pat Robertson and Corrie ten Boom. In addition, he fulfilled various editorial capacities for Christian magazines and was spiritual overseer of the Tabernacle Church in Melbourne, Florida.

Most of all, Jamie wrote to motivate Christians to go deeper and higher into a life with God. That is the purpose of this devotional, drawn from a few of his books that underscored the promise of God's power for our lives.

"I have written to urge you to attempt the impossible, to run the risk of failure, to dare to praise, to dare to love, to dare to die to self," explained Jamie. "I have written in hopes you will become the person you are—which is the essence of salvation—and to know the joy, the thrill, of letting the Holy Spirit control your life as you soar like the eagle through the tough ventures of life."[3]

*—Judith Couchman,*
*July 1997*

1. Jamie Buckingham, *Where Eagles Soar* (Old Tappan, N.J.: Chosen Books, 1980), 122.
2. Buckingham, 129.
3. Buckingham, 206.

## PART ONE

## WALKING WITH GOD

But you will not mind the roughness nor the
    steepness of the way,
Nor the chill, unrested morning, nor the searness
    of the day;
And you will not take a turning to the left nor to the
    right,
But go straight ahead, nor tremble at the coming
    of the night,
For the road leads home.

AUTHOR UNKNOWN

And though the Lord give you the bread of adversity,
and the water of affliction, yet shall not thy teachers be
removed into a corner any more, but thine eyes shall
see thy teachers. And thine ears shall hear a word
behind thee, saying, "This is the way, walk ye in it,
when ye turn to the right hand, and when ye turn to
the left."

ISAIAH 30:20-21, KJV

JAMIE BUCKINGHAM'S INSIGHT

The higher way of guidance is not to follow the Lord,
but to go before Him as He directs.
We need to tune our ears to the Voice behind us.

## THE BREATH OF GOD

### THOUGHT FOR TODAY

God fills and sustains us with the breath of His Spirit.

### WISDOM FROM SCRIPTURE

"To whom will you compare me? Or who is my equal?" says the Holy One.

Lift your eyes and look to the heavens: Who created all these? He who brings out the starry host one by one, and calls them each by name. Because of his great power and mighty strength, not one of them is missing.

Why do you say, O Jacob, and complain, O Israel, "My way is hidden from the Lord; my cause is disregarded by my God"?

Do you not know? Have you not heard? The Lord is the everlasting God, the Creator of the ends of the earth. He will not grow tired or weary, and his understanding no one can fathom.

He gives strength to the weary and increases the power of the weak.

Even youths grow tired and weary, and young men stumble and fall; but those who hope in the Lord will renew their strength. They will soar on wings like eagles; they will run and not grow weary, they will walk and not be faint.

ISAIAH 40:25-31, NIV

# Insights From Jamie Buckingham

"Watch the eagle," our Israeli guide said, pointing high above the Sinai Desert at the silent figure, soaring close to the mountains. "He locks his wings, pics the thermals, and rides the breath of God above the storm."

We were near the summit of the seven thousand, six hundred foot mountain, and the eagle was nearly ten thousand feet above us. And climbing.

"That's what the prophet meant when he said God's people would mount up with wings as eagles," the tough, dark-skinned Israeli said as he squatted on the pathway, waiting for the rest of the men to catch up.

"How high will he go?" I asked.

"Over the storm. Twenty-five, thirty thousand feet. He is now beyond his own control. He locks his wings, here," he said—pointing at his shoulders—"and rides the wind of God."

Again he used the magnificent Hebrew word *ruach* to describe the thermals of the desert. It was the same word King David used in Psalm 51 to describe the Holy Spirit— the breath of God. "Take not thy *ruach* from me."

In the New Testament the word is softer, more gentle. There we find the Greek word *pneuma,* meaning breath or spirit. It is the same word from which we get "pneumatic." In the New Testament it is often used to describe a filling experience. So the Holy Spirit fills, much as one would blow air into a balloon. The thought is one of lifting—from within. But in the Old Testament, the Spirit of God, the *ruach,* is anything but gentle. Here it is a roaring wind, howling through the canyons and moaning over the mountains. It is the mighty winds of the storms blowing across the wilderness accompanied by flashing lightning and rumbling thunder. It is the hot air thermals rushing upward. And upon it rides the eagle, ascending to unbelievable heights, using the air currents which destroy things on the ground to carry him over the fury of the storm to safety on the other side.

"He fears nothing," the guide said as we rose to greet the other men. "Even though we no longer see him, he can see us. He can see for fifty miles. He will go so high he will be covered with ice—his head, his wings, everything. Then he descends on the backside of the storm and the ice melts. Who knows? If it were not for the ice, he might just keep going up, touch God and never come down."

It's interesting how I keep thinking of that eagle—and the breath of God upon which he rides. I think of his determination, in the face of impossible odds, to lock his wings so that nothing can deter him from his upward climb.

It has been several years since I had that exhilarating experience the Bible describes as the baptism in the Holy Spirit. For a while I was able to stay spiritually airborne on the enthusiasm alone. "Enthusiasm," by the way, comes from two Greek words, *en theos,* meaning "in God." But if the Christian walk is merely enthusiasm, we become nothing more than spiritual grasshoppers, going up and down but never learning how to soar. I need more than being "in God." I must have God in me. Once airborne, I need some power to keep me aloft.

It was then I discovered there was more to the Christian life than living on experiences. Being born again is an experience. Being healed is an experience. Being baptized in the Holy Spirit is an experience. But if the experience does not open the door to an ongoing process, then we soon fall to earth again—battered, flattened and often in worse shape than when we made our upward leap.

Conversion—turning your back on a self-centered way of life and allowing Jesus Christ to take total control—is an experience. But a person needs more than conversion—he or she needs salvation, which is an ongoing process. Salvation, in its truest sense, is becoming who we really are. And that process is never complete—at least not here on earth.

The Spirit-controlled life is an ongoing process. It consists not only of allowing the breath of God to fill and expand you to the proper size and shape, but it consists of allowing the wind of God to bear you aloft—and keep you there. The *ruach* not only controls your path of flight in the face of oncoming storms, but He enables you to search the exalted corridors of heaven and brush your wings against the face of God.

There are certain things you must do, however, before that is possible. For one, you must recognize who you are. You are an eagle, not a grasshopper. Then you must be willing to cooperate with God, to put yourself in takeoff position for God to fill you—and send you soaring. To remain on your nest when the storm blows is disastrous. Your only hope is to launch out in faith against all insurmountable obstacles, lock your wings, and let God do the rest.

—*Where Eagles Soar*

## QUESTIONS TO CONSIDER
1. Is your Christian walk based on experience, or on knowing God?
2. How can you place yourself in "takeoff position" for soaring with Him?

## A PRAYERFUL RESPONSE
Lord, I totally commit my life to You. Amen.

---

## FINDING YOUR PLACE

### THOUGHT FOR TODAY

Our eternal home, our place, is in heaven.

### WISDOM FROM SCRIPTURE

Keep me safe, O God, for in you I take refuge.

I said to the Lord, "You are my Lord; apart from you I have no good thing."

As for the saints who are in the land, they are the glorious ones in whom is all my delight.

The sorrows of those will increase who run after other gods. I will not pour out their libations of blood or take up their names on my lips.

Lord, you have assigned me my portion and my cup; you have made my lot secure.

The boundary lines have fallen for me in pleasant places; surely I have a delightful inheritance.

I will praise the Lord, who counsels me; even at night my heart instructs me.

I have set the Lord always before me. Because he is at my right hand, I will not be shaken.

Therefore my heart is glad and my tongue rejoices; my body also will rest secure, because you will not abandon me to the grave, nor will you let your Holy One see decay.

You have made known to me the path of life; you will fill me with joy in your presence, with eternal pleasures at your right hand.

PSALM 16, NIV

## Insights From Jamie Buckingham

Recently I visited the home of an old man who had been in the nursery and greenhouse business all his life. "I'm an author, too," he said seriously.

"Oh, I didn't know."

"Oh, yes," he said, pointing to a yellowed clipping that had been framed behind glass and hung near the fireplace next to an award for growing the finest nasturtiums for the county fair. I walked over to the frame. It was a letter to the editor giving an opinion on why people should not vote for Franklin D. Roosevelt for a third term for president. His name was printed at the bottom.

It was his place.

We see it in church—this desire to belong. "If I can only be elected president of my Sunday school class." "At last, I've been elected as a deacon." Or, "Hey, everybody! I'm the person who washes the communion glasses."

How do we find our place?

First, we find it by confessing we are lost and looking. Salvation is a process that starts at an experience and continues for the rest of our earthly lives. There is a sense in which things are settled, finished, at salvation. This is true for our eternal security, for instance. But when it comes to finding our place on earth—to moving into maturity—then salvation is a process that continues until death. It is a never-ending process—this process of being saved.

Second, we find our place by recognizing the basic difference between a citizen and a tourist. A citizen has a sense of permanency, a sense of belonging. If you are a citizen, you buy a home. You settle down. You register and vote. You may even run for public office. You buy a cemetery plot. You put your name on the end of a pew. That is your home.

But citizens of God's kingdom are a different lot. This earth is not their home. They are just passing through. They are pilgrims. They keep their eternal passport in their pockets at all times.

That is the reason God warns His people against being unequally yoked with unbelievers, about being in debt to no man, about staying clear of the world systems that put us in bondage. God doesn't want us with roots so deep in the earth that when the trumpet sounds, we can't go.

When you are a pilgrim—when you are just passing through—you put a much lower value on material possessions. Things are to be used for God's glory, but not hoarded. We are to possess them, not let them possess us. Material possessions are not wrong, but they must not occupy the premium place in our lives. Possessions are to be used for God's glory, not misused for selfish reasons.

Third, one never finds his or her place until he or she enters the kingdom with utter abandonment, slamming the door forever on materialistic and selfish goals as a way of life.

Several years ago, driving through Norfolk, Virginia, I pulled up at a stoplight beside a big yellow school bus filled with nuns. Glancing out my window, I saw written on the side of the bus, "Sisters of Divine Providence."

I thought, *That's great. A whole busload of people living on faith—divine providence.*

Then the bus pulled out in front of me, and on the back door it said, in much smaller letters, "Emergency Exit."

People of divine providence have no emergency exits. Trusting God means sealing up all the other ways out. It's like those teenager friends of Daniel who said to Nebuchadnezzar, "O king, we will not serve thy gods, for our God is able to deliver us from the fiery furnace. But even if He doesn't intervene, we'll still not disobey Him" (see Dn 3:16-18).

To them, trusting God meant sealing off all emergency exits. And so it does with today's pilgrims. It means welding all the doors shut. It means burning all bridges so we cannot go back. It means turning your back on everything but the tabernacles of God.

—*Where Eagles Soar*

## QUESTIONS TO CONSIDER
1. What is your "place" in life?
2. How can you increasingly find your place in the tabernacles of God?

## A PRAYERFUL RESPONSE
Lord, I will seek to find my place in You. Amen.

## THE JOY AND DANGER OF DISCOVERY

### THOUGHT FOR TODAY

Abundant life means risking all to follow God's call.

### WISDOM FROM SCRIPTURE

Simon Peter answered, "You are the Christ, the Son of the living God."

Jesus replied, "Blessed are you, Simon son of Jonah, for this was not revealed to you by man, but by my Father in heaven.

"And I tell you that you are Peter, and on this rock I will build my church, and the gates of Hades will not overcome it.

"I will give you the keys of the kingdom of heaven; whatever you bind on earth will be bound in heaven, and whatever you loose on earth will be loosed in heaven."

Then he warned his disciples not to tell anyone that he was the Christ.

From that time on Jesus began to explain to his disciples that he must go to Jerusalem and suffer many things at the hands of the elders, chief priests and teachers of the law, and that he must be killed and on the third day be raised to life.

Peter took him aside and began to rebuke him. "Never, Lord!" he said. "This shall never happen to you!"

Jesus turned and said to Peter, "Get behind me, Satan! You are a stumbling block to me; you do not have in mind the things of God, but the things of men."

Then Jesus said to his disciples, "If anyone would come after me, he must deny himself and take up his cross and follow me.

"For whoever wants to save his life will lose it, but whoever loses his life for me will find it.

"What good will it be for a man if he gains the whole world, yet forfeits his soul? Or what can a man give in exchange for his soul?

"For the Son of Man is going to come in his Father's glory with his angels, and then he will reward each person according to what he has done."

MATTHEW 16:16-27, NIV

## INSIGHTS FROM JAMIE BUCKINGHAM

The desire to belong—to find a place—is basic in our nature. However, the Spirit-filled person will never be content to remain caged, despite the safety that bars seem to provide. Once aloft on the winds of God, the spirit of a person is activated to adventure. It will never be satisfied unless it is moving upward—exploring, discovering, venturing.

But daring to live the venturesome life of the eagle is risky business. When Jesus closed the book in the synagogue in Nazareth and sat down—after having defined His purpose—the religious people rose up in furor and tried to kill Him. He had threatened them by saying He was leaving the ruts and heading out across forbidden territory.

It's dangerous out there. And sometimes lonely. Yet, as Kipling said in "The Explorer," there is a voice beyond the mountains calling, which somehow keeps us going, pioneering, searching. Thus, despite our timidity, our hesitancy, our proneness to make mistakes, we know there is more, much more than we have experienced in our dusty ruts of traditional religion. The call of spiritual adventure grows louder the closer we move to God. So we venture out.

There is a place in the Christian community for the dreamer. Most of us dream dreams, however, then put them aside as impossible. Yet God never puts a desire in our heart, or beckons us to walk on water, unless He intends for us to step out on faith and at least make the attempt. Whether we achieve or not is almost immaterial; the passing of the test lies in whether we try, in whether we're willing to be obedient to the inner call to greatness—the onward call to spiritual adventure.

Every child of God has a promised mountain in his or her life. It may be a childhood dream or vision. It may be a teenage desire that has now been tossed aside as too impossible. It may be something God gave in prayer that seemed so impractical it was never tried. It may be a seemingly insurmountable obstacle. But every child of God has a promised mountain.

It's easy to be content with the valleys. Ruts have great appeal. If it's not giants on the mountain, it's mines under the sand. So people snuggle in ecclesiastical gowns, bury themselves in their libraries of musty books, build the cathedrals, draw charts of end times, but never venture out into the arena of the impossible, never taste of new wine, much less experiment with a new wineskin.

My friend Roger Wilson says he is building his life and his family so that if the Holy Spirit were ever removed, everything would fall apart.

That's real mountain climbing.

That's the way churches need to be built: so if the Spirit of God is ever removed, the walls will fall down, the roof will cave in, the money will disappear and all the people will leave.

I have a printed sign, in a big frame, which hangs above my desk. It says, "Attempt something so big that unless God intervenes it is bound to fail."

That, too, is mountain climbing.

Do not despair of those childhood dramas, those visions that came in adolescence. They are the fiber of life, the stuff that holds us together. Dangerous? To be sure. Foolish? Never.

In the Buckingham house we are challenging our children to invest their futures in things that will cost them their lives—for the glory of God. We are challenging them to go out, even at an early age, and be willing to die for Jesus.

The world does not understand this philosophy. The world says, "Be in control." But God says, "Be out of control." The world says parents should protect their children from death, not point them toward it. But we know there is no glory anywhere outside that which is done strictly for the glory of God. Abundant life comes only when we give our lives totally and completely to what God has called us.

—*Where Eagles Soar*

## QUESTIONS TO CONSIDER
1. What is the "promised mountain" in your life?
2. How can you pursue this dream?

## A PRAYERFUL RESPONSE
Lord, I will trust and not be afraid to pursue Your call. Amen.

## THE OTHER SIDE OF GOD

### THOUGHT FOR TODAY

As our loving Father, God wants to protect us from spiritual enemies.

### WISDOM FROM SCRIPTURE

Do not fret because of evil men or be envious of those who do wrong; for like the grass they will soon wither, like green plants they will soon die away.

Trust in the Lord and do good; dwell in the land and enjoy safe pasture.

Delight yourself in the Lord and he will give you the desires of your heart.

Commit your way to the Lord; trust in him and he will do this:

He will make your righteousness shine like the dawn, the justice of your cause like the noonday sun.

Be still before the Lord and wait patiently for him; do not fret when men succeed in their ways, when they carry out their wicked schemes.

Refrain from anger and turn from wrath; do not fret—it leads only to evil.

For evil men will be cut off, but those who hope in the Lord will inherit the land.

A little while, and the wicked will be no more; though you look for them, they will not be found.

But the meek will inherit the land and enjoy great peace.

PSALM 37:1-11, NIV

## INSIGHTS FROM JAMIE BUCKINGHAM

Most of us have a very low concept of God. We believe He can fail us. We believe we can slip from His grasp and fall into hell—even after He has committed Himself to us. We believe we can offend Him, and He will cast us out. We judge His love for us on the basis of earthman's love for his children. We do not understand His patience, His love, His mercy, His grace, His provision, His protection, His healing power, His glory. We cannot comprehend how He welcomes, even invites us into His presence, despite our sins. There is so much about Him we do not know.

How desperately we need to know Him as Father, remembering there are more sides to Him than we will ever recognize. To us He may be love and grace. But to our enemies He may be a roaring vengeance that causes them to quake.

The prophet Nahum gives us brilliant insight into this other side of God, helping us enlarge our vision and understand there is so much about Him that is incomprehensible.

Once before, God had sent a prophet to the city of Nineveh. The first to go was the reluctant prophet Jonah. God said He loved the Assyrians, however, and was eager to bless them. But He could not bless them unless they repented of their evil as individuals and as a nation. So the Lord sent the Hebrew prophet Jonah to the capital city of Assyria to call the people to repentance. They did repent, from the king to the lowest peasant.

God honored their repentance and blessed the nation for 150 years. But after five generations, the nation once again slipped into idolatry and wickedness. They became the destroyer of the people of God, the archenemy of the people of Judah. Once again God sent a prophet. Nahum went to speak the word of God to the wicked nation. Only this time it was not a call to repentance, it was a cry of vengeance. God was angry at the Assyrians for humiliating and destroying His chosen people, Israel, and promised to destroy them.

Here is our Father with His finger against the chest of the enemy. No more shall they curse and humiliate and destroy the children of God. This time the Assyrians were not just dealing with children, they were face-to-face with the Almighty God, the Creator of the Universe, and His wrath was mighty to behold. Yet that night, back in the Father's house, God had only words of peace and comfort for His children, Judah.

God has two faces—one that is presented to those who would harm and destroy His children, and one He presents to His children. In the book of Nahum we see the other side of God, a God of terror to His enemies, who destroys them with His mighty arm and the flame of His wrath. But at the same time, He reaches out in tender mercy to those who would trust Him, to those who would turn to Him for help.

In our desire to discover the person of God, we need to see Him standing against our enemies. Who are the enemies of God's children? Disease. Deception. Sin. Demonic forces. Satan. When these come against the people of God, our loving heavenly Father builds up a storm, and He rides that storm with the host of heaven against the entrenched forces, and He grinds the seed of Satan to the earth, and He utterly destroys those things that would oppose Him. He is God, and there is no force in the world capable of destroying Him or destroying His church.

There are occasions when I want to step into all the pulpits of the world, to cry from every steeple, to stand on the balconies and stages of the nations and shout: "Live your vision. Know Him! Do not be afraid He will destroy you. He wants to take over your life and bring you meaning and purpose."

We have a great God. We do not need to fear what is happening in His kingdom. We need to be willing to move out beyond our own control so He can be in total control. God does not have to be convinced to be separated from His blessings; He wants to bless all His people. He wants to bless every church. And in the midst of the blessings, He will protect His children from evil.

Moses came outside the tabernacle, lifted his hand in the air and cried with a great voice, "Let God arise! and His enemies be scattered!"

That cry still echoes through the corridors of time as the enemies of God are scattered before the mighty power of His Holy Spirit. That is the reason I am not afraid.

There is no fear when we approach God through His Son, Jesus. God is our daddy. He loves us. He is protecting us. And even though His hand may be against our backside on occasion, it is not there to punish but to direct. His voice is constantly saying, "This is the way, walk ye in it."

—*Where Eagles Soar*

## QUESTIONS TO CONSIDER
1. When have you seen the two faces of God?
2. Which "face" do you want to know better? Why?

## A PRAYERFUL RESPONSE
Lord, thank You for being a loving, protective Father. Amen.

# DAY 5

## ABIDING IN THE SHADOW

### THOUGHT FOR TODAY
Knowing God requires abiding in His presence.

### WISDOM FROM SCRIPTURE
He who dwells in the shelter of the Most High will rest in the shadow of the Almighty.

I will say of the Lord, "He is my refuge and my fortress, my God, in whom I trust."

Surely he will save you from the fowler's snare and from the deadly pestilence.

He will cover you with his feathers, and under his wings you will find refuge; his faithfulness will be your shield and rampart.

You will not fear the terror of night, nor the arrow that flies by day, nor the pestilence that stalks in the darkness, nor the plague that destroys at midday.

A thousand may fall at your side, ten thousand at your right hand, but it will not come near you.

You will only observe with your eyes and see the punishment of the wicked.

If you make the Most High your dwelling—even the Lord, who is my refuge—then no harm will befall you, no disaster will come near your tent.

For he will command his angels concerning you to guard you in all your ways; they will lift you up in their hands, so that you will not strike your foot against a stone.

PSALM 91:1-12, NIV

## INSIGHTS FROM JAMIE BUCKINGHAM

My wife, Jackie, knows if I spend the night at someone's house I will invariably go through their closet before the night is over, rummaging through all the stuff on the shelf, opening boxes and drawers. If I use their bathroom I will peek in the medicine cabinet, open the linen closet and look under the sink.

Why? Because I want to know people, and the only way to do that is to get beneath the guest towels and fancy pillowcases and see how they live when I'm not around. You can discover a great deal about people by opening their refrigerator and checking their bookshelf; for what people eat and read is a good barometer to their personality and character.

But you cannot know God by just opening His closet or reading His Book. For God is immortal, and we are made of different stuff. Simply going to church and hearing about Him, taking the sacraments, singing His hymns, reading the Bible—even if we memorize it in its entirety—will not open the door of knowledge to God. That comes only when you abide in His presence. But such a relationship is not formed overnight. It takes a lifetime. And beyond.

The lovable Dutch woman, Corrie ten Boom, once taught me something about abiding with God. She was in our home while I was working on *Tramp for the Lord*. We had reached a difficult place in the book, and our personalities had crossed. I thought she should go in one direction, but she was determined the book should go in another. I was terribly frustrated, and I finally confronted her.

"Tante Corrie, you do a great deal of talking about walking in the light, but I don't see any light now. All you have done is walk over me in this matter. I want to go one way, and you are a stubborn old Dutch woman who insists we go another. I don't think you're walking in the light at all."

It was a difficult thing for me to say to a woman whom much of Christendom revered as not only a living legend but as a literal saint. She looked at me, gave me her old Dutch smile and shared with me the secret of Psalm 91:1, "He that dwelleth in the secret place of the most High shall abide under the shadow of the Almighty."

"There comes a time," she said, "when you don't walk in the light anymore."

"I do not understand."

"Well, you don't walk in the light when you are walking through the valley of the shadow, right? There is no light in the valley. All there is in the valley is the promise of His presence."

I understood that principle. I know the artificiality of lighthearted smiles and happy hallelujahs when a person is going through a period of deep darkness, grief or repentance. There are few genuine hallelujahs when all the lights go out.

"Neither can you walk in the light when you are abiding under the shadow," Corrie said, looking deep into my face. "The closer you get to God, the less you understand Him. But the more you believe Him."

Months after Corrie had gone, that nugget stayed with me. We are called to walk, not by sight, but by faith. The person who knows God nominally, who has a hat-tipping experience with Him, who meets Him twice a year at Easter and Christmas—that man or woman can tell you volumes about the nature and character of God. But come into the presence of a person who abides under the shadow, and all that person can say is, "Shhhh. Be still and abide." He knows very little. He just believes.

You can write a systematic theology, but you cannot diagram God. Neither can you draw out a schematic pattern of His kingdom. But he that dwells in the secret place of the most High, who abides under the shadow of His wings, does not walk by sight, he walks by faith. And that cannot be diagrammed—it can only be demonstrated.

I will never actually see God—at least this side of Glory—for His face is too much for me to behold. To His enemies He bares His arm, but His children hear only the soft sound of His voice behind, saying, "This is the way, walk ye in it."

The higher way of guidance is not to follow the Lord but to go before Him as He directs. He longs to bring His children into such maturity that they can walk alone. He does not desire to hold us with a tight rein as a horse or mule, but with freedom, guided only by His eye upon us. If at any moment we misstep, if our ear is tuned to His voice, He will speak softly and say, "No, not that way, this is the way—walk ye in it."

We need to tune our spiritual ears to the voice behind us.

—*Where Eagles Soar*

## QUESTIONS TO CONSIDER

1. How are you getting to know God?
2. What does abiding under the shadow of His wings mean to you?

## A PRAYERFUL RESPONSE

Lord, teach me to abide under the shadow of Your wings. Amen.

# DAY 6

## IN GOD'S HANDS

### THOUGHT FOR TODAY
God is the one in control of our lives.

### WISDOM FROM SCRIPTURE
In you, O Lord, I have taken refuge; let me never be put to shame; deliver me in your righteousness.

Turn your ear to me, come quickly to my rescue; be my rock of refuge, a strong fortress to save me.

Since you are my rock and my fortress, for the sake of your name lead and guide me.

Free me from the trap that is set for me, for you are my refuge.

Into your hands I commit my spirit; redeem me, O Lord, the God of truth.

I hate those who cling to worthless idols; I trust in the Lord.

I will be glad and rejoice in your love, for you saw my affliction and knew the anguish of my soul.

You have not handed me over to the enemy but have set my feet in a spacious place.

Be merciful to me, O Lord, for I am in distress; my eyes grow weak with sorrow, my soul and my body with grief.

My life is consumed by anguish and my years by groaning; my strength fails because of my affliction, and my bones grow weak.

Because of all my enemies, I am the utter contempt of my neighbors; I am a dread to my friends—those who see me on the street flee from me.

I am forgotten by them as though I were dead; I have become like broken pottery.

For I hear the slander of many; there is terror on every side; they conspire against me and plot to take my life.

But I trust in you, O Lord; I say, "You are my God."

My times are in your hands; deliver me from my enemies and from those who pursue me.

PSALM 31:1-15, NIV

## INSIGHTS FROM JAMIE BUCKINGHAM

Our times are indeed, as David said, in His hands. It is God who gives life and God who takes it away. There is no reason for us to walk through life with a chip on our shoulder or our fists balled up, anticipating a fight. People who go through life like that always meet someone ready to take on their challenge. The Romans used to say, *Si vis pacem, para bellum.* (If you wish peace, prepare for war.) This is still the theme of our Department of Defense.

But in the kingdom of God the very opposite is true. He who is servant is leader, he who is last is first, he who ministers peace is the strongest warrior. As God's children we can walk through this world unafraid, for our times are in His hands. He is in sovereign control of our lives and of this universe.

We often forget that. We forget it when we are tense, anxious, when the money runs out, when our job is terminated, when the doctor says we have cancer, when the little baby inside begins to try to get out. We forget that God is in control of His world—and especially His children.

There is an interesting story in Mark 4 that illustrates this. All day Jesus had been teaching along the shore of the

Sea of Galilee. When evening came, He asked His disciples, most of whom were fishermen and had their own boats, to take Him to the other side of the big lake. But His request was more than a suggestion; it was a positive affirmation. "Let us pass over unto the other side" (Mk 4:35).

Since all the disciples could not get in the one boat, they took several other smaller boats also. Jesus, who was physically tired, settled down in the stern of the boat, put His head on a pillow and went to sleep. As still happens on the Galilee, a great storm arose without any warning and suddenly the tiny ships were in danger of being capsized. Water was pouring in over the gunwales. The disciples were bailing, but it looked like the ships were going down. Seeing Jesus still asleep in the midst of this horrible storm, one of the men cried out: "Master, carest thou not that we perish?" It was a simple, human cry. "Master, do something!"

Jesus woke up. Seeing the fear on the faces of the disciples, He spoke to the sea: "Peace, be still." Immediately the wind ceased to blow, the huge waves subsided and the storm was over.

Then turning to His followers, Jesus rebuked them. "Why all this fear? Have you no faith?"

That remark used to bother me, for it seemed to be an unjust rebuke. Who wouldn't be afraid in a situation like that? But you cannot understand unless you remember Christ's words. Before they embarked, Jesus had affirmed: "We're going to the other side."

Faith is believing God will do what He says, regardless of the height of the waves. Fear causes us to look at the circumstances. Faith causes us to look at God. It is the gift that enables us to go to sleep in the middle of a storm, knowing God has promised we will cross over—knowing God is in total control.

As the ongoing ministry of Jesus, not only do we have faith to believe God's Word will bring us through, but we have the authority to speak to the elements—just as Jesus did—if they get in the way of God's intent and purpose.

Spiritual authority is one of the attributes that accompanies salvation and the Spirit-controlled life, yet it is so seldom used. How vividly I remember the reply Corrie ten Boom gave when asked about a certain missionary family who was under great attack on the mission field, harassed by circumstances, defeated by sickness, plagued by evil spirits. The fabled old Dutch woman shook her head sadly. "They have given all, but they have not taken all."

How desperately we need to take the authority God has given us and defeat the enemies that surround us.

—*Where Eagles Soar*

## QUESTIONS TO CONSIDER
1. In what ways do you need to trust God's control of your life?
2. How can you take hold of your spiritual authority?

## A PRAYERFUL RESPONSE
Lord, even though the storm is fierce, I will believe Your promises. Amen.

## Let Your Dreams Come True

### Thought for Today
God wants to fulfill the dreams He places in our hearts.

### Wisdom From Scripture
Now there was a man in Jerusalem called Simeon, who was righteous and devout. He was waiting for the consolation of Israel, and the Holy Spirit was upon him.

It had been revealed to him by the Holy Spirit that he would not die before he had seen the Lord's Christ.

Moved by the Spirit, he went into the temple courts. When the parents brought in the child Jesus to do for him what the custom of the Law required, Simeon took him in his arms and praised God, saying: "Sovereign Lord, as you have promised, you now dismiss your servant in peace.

"For my eyes have seen your salvation, which you have prepared in the sight of all people, a light for revelation to the Gentiles and for glory to your people Israel."

The child's father and mother marveled at what was said about him.

Then Simeon blessed them and said to Mary, his mother: "This child is destined to cause the falling and rising of many in Israel, and to be a sign that will be spoken against, so that the thoughts of many hearts will be revealed. And a sword will pierce your own soul too."

There was also a prophetess, Anna, the daughter of Phanuel, of the tribe of Asher. She was very old; she had lived with her husband seven years after her marriage, and then was a widow until she was eighty-four. She never left the temple but worshiped night and day, fasting and praying.

Coming up to them at that very moment, she gave thanks to God and spoke about the child to all who were looking forward to the redemption of Jerusalem.

LUKE 2:25-38, NIV

## INSIGHTS FROM JAMIE BUCKINGHAM

Everyone has at least one basic dream—something we believe God has laid on our hearts, something that has not yet come to pass, but which we fervently believe will happen one day. To the believer whose life has moved into the Spirit's control, the fulfillment of dreams is a profound venture.

Some people have already experienced the realization, the fulfillment, of a dream. They are the happy ones. But to most of us the fulfillment of our dream is still far off. My friend says happy people are those who know they are at least moving toward the fulfillment of their dream. The unhappy, frustrated ones are those who feel their dream has passed them by or that what they long for is impossible. They are the ones who believe life is only a cruel trick, a design to make a mockery of the desires of our hearts.

But the dreams God places in our hearts are all attainable. Grace is the supernatural power God gives the believer to accomplish His will, to bring those dreams to pass. This is difficult for us to grasp, for we have been conditioned to believe that if we do not bring a thing to pass in our own strength, it will not come to pass. But if we are the living, breathing, acting, loving extension of the man Jesus Christ in the world today, then the things He did, we can do also.

His mission is now our mission; His dream, ours.

There are two kinds of dreams: those we dream up ourselves, which are nearly always self-centered, and those God places in our hearts. God gives each one of us the desire to accomplish His will, to fulfill the dreams He places in our hearts, and the power to do it. But the only legitimate dreams are the ones God places in our hearts.

The Holy Spirit accomplishes His work in this world by the measure of faith each man is given to express his personal spiritual gift. It is the process He uses to make the dream He has placed in our hearts come true. This is best understood when we realize that our loving God has created each one of us to do best that which we enjoy doing. Whatever it is, the Potter has designed something into each one of us that needs to be sanctified, some special gift that when discovered and put into use will bring happiness and satisfaction by fulfilling the desire of our hearts.

The kind of dream I am talking about—your deepest hope, the desire of your heart—will not grow up overnight. Such a dream has to materialize, evolve, go through process after process until it is matured. Remember, you may have only one dream for a lifetime. That dream may hit several plateaus along the way, but for most of us there is only one basic dream per person. It is the wise person who is able to focus in and know what that is, to define it exactly.

If you have but one dream to a lifetime, then it's worth waiting a lifetime for it to come to pass. Simeon waited all his life to see the fulfillment of his highest dream—that his eyes would see the Messiah. Doubtless he had been tricked many times before. Surely people had pointed out great leaders and whispered, "That's the Messiah." But there had been no inner witness of the Spirit. So Simeon waited. Like Abraham and Sarah, who waited into old age for the fulfillment of God's promise of a child, hope had nearly faded away. But Simeon held on to his dream. And then one day in the Temple, going about his daily worship as he had for decades, his dream came true.

If Jesus Christ is Lord, then He can do with you what He chooses. To bring you to that place where the dream He has placed within your heart can come to pass, He often has to do a great deal of reshaping. That sometimes causes pain, humiliation, even death. Sometimes it means we are bruised or scratched. We can choose to blame Satan when we undergo tough times if we want, but if our dream is legitimate—if it comes from God—then it is not the devil who is twisting our life but the Holy Spirit. God allows these things to come into your life for the purpose of making you a fit container for His dream. Plastic surgery is often painful, especially when it is done in public, but at the same time it is necessary if we are to reflect God's grace.

So the question remains for all of us: Can we release even our dreams to God, to let them come to pass in His time and His way—not ours?

It's a venture we shouldn't miss.

—*Where Eagles Soar*

## QUESTIONS TO CONSIDER

1. What is the dream that God has placed in your heart?
2. Are you willing to do whatever it takes, even wait a lifetime, for it to come true?

## A PRAYERFUL RESPONSE

Lord, I will wait for Your timing for the dreams in my heart. Amen.

# DAY 8

## THE JONAH COMPLEX

### THOUGHT FOR TODAY
Our anger doesn't accomplish God's purposes.

### WISDOM FROM SCRIPTURE
As a prisoner for the Lord, then, I urge you to live a life worthy of the calling you have received.

Be completely humble and gentle; be patient, bearing with one another in love.

Make every effort to keep the unity of the Spirit through the bond of peace.

There is one body and one Spirit—just as you were called to one hope when you were called—one Lord, one faith, one baptism; one God and Father of all, who is over all and through all and in all.

But to each one of us grace has been given as Christ apportioned it.

You were taught, with regard to your former way of life, to put off your old self, which is being corrupted by its deceitful desires; to be made new in the attitude of your minds; and to put on the new self, created to be like God in true righteousness and holiness.

Therefore each of you must put off falsehood and speak truthfully to his neighbor, for we are all members of one body.

In your anger do not sin: Do not let the sun go down while you are still angry, and do not give the devil a foothold.

EPHESIANS 4:1-7, 22-27, NIV

## Insights From Jamie Buckingham

The book of Jonah is a short book. Four chapters long. Most of the story is familiar—Jonah receiving a call from God to preach in Nineveh; his running from God. The incident aboard the ship when he is finally thrown overboard. That infamous whale. Then Jonah picking himself up off the beach and reeking of seaweed and caviar, heading out to Nineveh to preach the Word of the Lord.

It seems that when a prophet with seaweed in his hair shows up and preaches repentance, people take him seriously. Not only did the people repent, but so did the king. They all put on sackcloth and smeared themselves in ashes, and God honored their repentance and withheld His judgment.

Then Jonah went outside the city, and that's where the difficult part of the story commences. Jonah was angry. He was angry because his theology had been shaken. It seems Jonah, the Jew, felt that all Assyrians deserved to be destroyed. In fact, he was hoping they would not repent and he could sit outside the city and watch as God wiped them out with fire and brimstone. When the destruction was withheld, however, Jonah grew angry and cried out to God to take his life.

One of the best ways to discover what a person is really like is to discover what makes him or her angry. I guess that was the reason, at one point in our marriage, my wife wanted me to read about Jonah—because it seems his anger was simply evidence of some other things inside him that were all messed up.

I paused as I read, thinking about a recent incident. It was just one of many, for I get angry at a lot of things. Big things seldom make me angry. It is the little things that cause me to blow my top. Just let someone scratch the surface of my life, upset my pet plan, disrupt my routine, interfere with my ... everything seemed to be centered around the word *my*. Just as it was with Jonah.

He had come to Nineveh with a chip on his shoulder. He was prejudiced. He had hated the Assyrians all of his life. After all, the Jews were God's chosen people—not the Arabs. Had it not been for that storm at sea and God's indisputable direction for his life, he would have been safe in Tarshish. Even so, he arrived in Nineveh convinced he was right and they were wrong. He could not handle it when they became right, too.

So there was Jonah, sitting under a big leafy gourd vine God had caused to grow up almost instantaneously to give him shade. Now Jonah was angry again. This time because a big green worm came along, ate the vine and cursed it to die, taking away his shade.

No wonder Jackie wanted me to read the last chapter of Jonah. That could have been me, sitting out there in the hot Assyrian sun. I'm angry at the Assyrians because they repented. I'm angry at God for not wiping them out. I'm angry at the worm, I'm angry at myself because I can't control my anger.

How like Jonah I was. How unlike Jesus.

Anger is an effect. And for every effect there is a cause. The cause of anger is not hate. The basic cause of anger is fear. Our anger is a face we raise to hide our insecurities. So when Paul tells Timothy that God has not given us a spirit of fear but of power and of love and of a sound mind, he wipes out all the reasons for self-anger.

People who are offended easily, who are edgy when someone or something rubs them the wrong way, who put up angry defense mechanisms, are usually very insecure, self-centered individuals. We don't want people getting close to us for fear they will discover what we are really like. Discovering that, we are afraid they won't like us any more. It is easier just to get angry.

As Christians come together in community, true *koinonia,* there will be even more rubbing and touching. We often reject this, afraid that if we are rubbed hard enough, others will discover we are only a thin veneer or that we're hollow inside. But it is only when the masks come off, when the outer layers are discarded, that we can be filled—and eventually, controlled—by the Holy Spirit. The purpose of our being rubbed and sandpapered and chiseled is not to expose us but to open us. A person cannot expand in the Spirit if he has nineteen coats of pain on him. Wineskins with that kind of covering never can hold the effervescing new wine.

Crusty people, those who get angry easily, are usually stiff and unbending. They have no elasticity. When confronted with situations they cannot handle, they blow up. Blood vessels in their head pop. Or their heart explodes. Or a stomach or colon ruptures or develops an ulcer. The Holy Spirit, however, is the Spirit of health. His desire, in controlling us, is to bring us to that place where everything works in harmony with the Lord of the universe—our heavenly Father.

Anger is a barrier that blocks relationships. But until I can identify it as such, I will not be able to relate correctly to those I wish to heal. Thus I must constantly ask myself if I am willing to undergo periods of discomfort, even make myself vulnerable to pain and death, in order to bring about change. In this case you can, by a deliberate act, expose yourself to the power of the Holy Spirit who will take that which you cannot control, bring it under His control and use it as a tool for the glory of God.

—*Where Eagles Soar*

## QUESTIONS TO CONSIDER
1. Do you suffer from the Jonah Complex? If so, why?
2. How can you allow the Holy Spirit to bring your anger under control?

## A PRAYERFUL RESPONSE
Lord, bring my anger under Your control for Your glory. Amen.

## Through the Fire

### Thought for Today

To be useful to God, we must pass through the Refiner's fire.

### Wisdom from Scripture

You have wearied the Lord with your words. "How have we wearied him?" you ask. By saying, "All who do evil are good in the eyes of the Lord, and he is pleased with them" or "Where is the God of justice?"

"See, I will send my messenger, who will prepare the way before me. Then suddenly the Lord you are seeking will come to his temple; the messenger of the covenant, whom you desire, will come," says the Lord Almighty.

But who can endure the day of his coming? Who can stand when he appears? For he will be like a refiner's fire or a launderer's soap.

He will sit as a refiner and purifier of silver; he will purify the Levites and refine them like gold and silver. Then the Lord will have men who will bring offerings in righteousness, and the offerings of Judah and Jerusalem will be acceptable to the Lord, as in days gone by, as in former years.

"So I will come near to you for judgment. I will be quick to testify against sorcerers, adulterers and perjurers, against those who defraud laborers of their wages, who oppress the widows and the fatherless, and deprive aliens of justice, but do not fear me," says the Lord Almighty.

"I the Lord do not change. So you, O descendants of Jacob, are not destroyed.

"Ever since the time of your forefathers you have turned away from my decrees and have not kept them. Return to me, and I will return to you," says the Lord Almighty.

MALACHI 2:17–3:7, NIV

## INSIGHTS FROM JAMIE BUCKINGHAM

When I had an encounter with the Holy Spirit—who, up until that time, I only recognized as a boring phrase in the doxology—almost everything about me was revolutionized instantly. All that has happened since is material for other volumes. The important point I want to make here is, I had nothing to do with it.

Everything in me had been striving against God. Like Jacob at Peniel, I had been vainly wrestling with the angel of the Lord, trying to have my own way, yet at the same time unwilling to turn loose until He blessed me. Now the blessing had come. And with it, a limp. Yet the limp—and the scars from an adulterous past—are badges for His glory.

Perfection still eludes me. I am still vulnerable. But most important, I am no longer satisfied with my imperfection. Nor, thank God, am I intimidated by it. I have reached the point of recognizing that God uses imperfect, immoral, dishonest people. In fact, that's all there are these days. All the holy people seem to have gone off and died. There's no one left but us sinners to carry on the ministry.

If I had my way I would never do anything wrong. Yet, like Paul, I say: "For I know that in me [that is, in my flesh] dwelleth no good thing; for to will is present with me, but how to perform that which is good I find not" (Rom 7:18, KJV).

Dissatisfied with imperfection, I am now determined to move toward the goal of "conforming to Christ," knowing at the same time it will never come because of my obedience but out of my submission to the Holy Spirit. It is that obedience which leads to the fine art of living beyond control—beyond self-will and into the comfort of the Spirit's control.

Malachi draws the picture of God sitting in front of the melting crucible under which burns the refiner's fire. The fire has been stoked to white heat. In the crucible is silver ore, representing, Malachi says, the "sons of Levi"—those chosen for special service in the kingdom. The fire is burning, purging the dross until only the pure metal is left. Only when the refiner peers into the crucible and sees the reflection of his own face is the heat turned down and the pure metal poured into the forms that bless the world.

My old friend Seabury Oliver says the only way a person—any person—ever comes to know God intimately is through trouble. Perhaps he's right. On the other hand, when I realize that most of my problems, perhaps all my problems, have been self-inflicted, I wonder if all this fire has been necessary. I suspect not. I look at others around me, those who have served God without the rebellious spirit that seems to be so much a part of my makeup, and see that they seem to have passed through the fire at very low temperatures and intensity. Without much pain or suffering they have come to a beautiful, simple, yet valid understanding of the deep truths of God. Others of us must pass through the Valley of the Shadow of Death before we can say with certainty, "My head is anointed. My cup runneth over."

Yet it is in these places, where the awful sins of life threaten to consume us, that we learn God can be trusted. Locking our wings in faith, we soar on the thermal of His Holy Spirit, out of control, yet in His will.

*—Where Eagles Soar*

## QUESTIONS TO CONSIDER
1. Are you passing through the Refiner's fire? If so, why would God be refining you?
2. How will you respond to God's refining process?

## A PRAYERFUL RESPONSE
Lord, refine me into an instrument that reflects Your face. Amen.

## Riding the Wind

### Thought for Today

If we're willing to risk, we can ride on the winds of the Spirit.

### Wisdom From Scripture

Praise the Lord, O my soul. O Lord my God, you are very great; you are clothed with splendor and majesty.

He wraps himself in light as with a garment; he stretches out the heavens like a tent and lays the beams of his upper chambers on their waters. He makes the clouds his chariot and rides on the wings of the wind.

He makes winds his messengers, flames of fire his servants.

He set the earth on its foundations; it can never be moved.

You covered it with the deep as with a garment; the waters stood above the mountains.

But at your rebuke the waters fled, at the sound of your thunder they took to flight; they flowed over the mountains, they went down into the valleys, to the place you assigned for them.

You set a boundary they cannot cross; never again will they cover the earth.

He makes springs pour water into the ravines; it flows between the mountains.

They give water to all the beasts of the field; the wild donkeys quench their thirst.

The birds of the air nest by the waters; they sing

among the branches.

He waters the mountains from his upper chambers; the earth is satisfied by the fruit of his work.

He makes grass grow for the cattle, and plants for man to cultivate—bringing forth food from the earth: wine that gladdens the heart of man, oil to make his face shine, and bread that sustains his heart.

PSALM 104:1-15, NIV

## INSIGHTS FROM JAMIE BUCKINGHAM

As long as I can remember there has been locked in my heart the desire to do daring things, to risk my life, so to speak, in adventure. But fear has locked the door on my venturing spirit—fear and self-imposed circumstances. The only times I dared step out were to clandestine things that only temporarily satisfied the driving desire to achieve, create, risk and dare. At the same time, though, I continued to yearn for a legitimate expression to that longing, some way to unlock the door of the cage of my soul so my spirit could soar like an eagle.

Still, I could in no way comprehend the immensity of what God had in store for me when I came face-to-face with who I was created to be. Jesus said that when the Holy Spirit comes into our lives He will lead us into all truth. Receiving Him is the greatest of all adventures. He is the key that unlocks the door of our inner being and allows our own spirit, that part of us breathed into us by the Father, to soar free—liberated.

The baptism of the Holy Spirit, though glorious, is also fraught with danger and risk. No longer will we ever be satisfied to feed our own spirit crumbs of fantasy and imagination. Having tasted the reality of God, we will be compelled to move upward, escaping the bonds of our carnal nature and taking on, more and more, the adventurous, daring attributes of God's Son, who was the greatest adventurer of all. For those few who are willing to risk all, to venture out, to die to self, there are precious and unique blessings ahead that the less venturesome will never experience.

Such blessings cannot be transmitted, only experienced; they are existential, not visionary; they cannot be given away, only enjoyed at the moment. Such experiences—and there will be innumerable ones for the Spirit-controlled individual—are like those fragile yet exquisite wildflowers sometimes found on the windswept pinnacle of a mountain. You stoop and examine, enjoy and are blessed by their symmetry, elegance and loveliness. How splendid is their form, how delicate their petals, how brilliant their color. The next day you return with a loved one, but the flowers are gone. They lasted but a day, and only the ones present at the hour they blossomed could experience and enjoy. They are God's gift to those who dare to venture out.

The Holy Spirit has unlocked the cage of my soul and allowed the eagle to ride the winds to the tops of mountains where I have tasted nectar I once thought reserved for God alone. I no longer have to fantasize, to daydream at my desk or sit in the evening staring at the fire, imagining romantic things. Since that grand unlocking years ago, life has been one continuing adventure. Those close to me are aware of my occasional slips back into carnality. But despite this, I know something has happened to me.

There are special blessings, I've learned, awaiting those who venture out. Authored in eternity, they break through into time and space only as men move upward toward God. They are never to be repeated, never to be shared, never to be wrapped in a package to be given away. They are like the blessings of breath: inhaled deeply, disseminated into the system and never to be recovered in form, only in energy.

Each step of the way God guides, leading us to new heights of adventure and experiences. The way may seem dangerous as we turn loose of all the safety devices of the past and set our faces toward the things of the Spirit; but there is a glorious reward, far more precious than the turquoise nuggets of the ancient mine, that awaits those who dare run the risk of discovery.

The joy of adventure remains only as long as God controls. When people step in with their reasons and fears to institutionalize and structure (or even record) that which is meant to flow free and unencumbered, life leaves. Yet it is this lack of institutionalizing that is the single factor preventing us from venturing out. How desperately the human soul wants to see a blueprint of the next step, to exert an element of control over what is about to happen. That is only our own humanity, which is afraid of the unknown, not that essence of God inside each of us.

It is the essence of God that urges us to dare, to release our towline to that mechanical device that has helped us break the elementary bonds of earth, and soar free on zephyrlike currents toward the dwelling place of the Most High.

—*Where Eagles Soar*

## Questions to Consider

1. Are you living in the light of all God created you to be? If not, why?
2. Are you willing to experience God's adventures for you? Why, or why not?

## A Prayerful Response

Lord, show me how to soar on the wings of Your Spirit. Amen.

## PART TWO

## LIVING BY FAITH

Lives of great men all remind us
We can make our lives sublime,
And, departing, leave behind us
Footprints on the sands of time;
Let us, then, be up and doing,
With a heart for any fate;
Still achieving, still pursuing,
Learn to labor and to wait.

HENRY WADSWORTH LONGFELLOW,
FROM "A PSALM OF LIFE"

Now faith is being sure of what we hope for and certain of what we do not see.

And without faith it is impossible to please God, because anyone who comes to him must believe that he exists and that he rewards those who earnestly seek him.

HEBREWS 11:1, 6, NIV

### JAMIE BUCKINGHAM'S INSIGHT
God uses ordinary people for His kingdom, if they are willing to obey and live by faith.

# DAY 11

## MAKING TOUGH DECISIONS

### THOUGHT FOR TODAY
Obeying God is the way to please Him.

### WISDOM FROM SCRIPTURE
The Lord said to Abram, after Lot had separated from him, "Raise your eyes now, and look from the place where you are, northward and southward and eastward and westward; for all the land that you see I will give to you and to your offspring forever.

"I will make your offspring like the dust of the earth; so that if one can count the dust of the earth, your offspring also can be counted.

"Rise up, walk through the length and the breadth of the land, for I will give it to you.

"I will indeed bless you, and I will make your offspring as numerous as the stars of heaven and as the sand that is on the seashore. And your offspring shall possess the gate of their enemies, and by your offspring shall all the nations of the earth gain blessing for themselves, because you have obeyed my voice."

GENESIS 13:14-17; 22:17-18, NRSV

### INSIGHTS FROM JAMIE BUCKINGHAM
In my wanderings through Israel I've discovered something about the people of the Bible. They really were people like you and me. They failed as well as succeeded. And they struggled with making tough decisions—the toughest being: Shall I obey God, or shall I do what I want to do?

If anyone was ever faced with tough decisions on obeying God it was Abram. No sooner would he get one thing settled than God would ask him to do something even harder; yet in every instance, he passed the test.

Abram was called a "Hebrew," which means pilgrim, nomad. Thus, when Lot said there was not room enough for the two of them, Abram chose once again to obey God. Jealous for the integrity of his tribe and its testimony before the corrupt society that was so closely observing him, he determined he should not dishonor God by causing disunity and conflict within his family—a family that had professed a loyalty to God, making them different from the pagans.

Abram's willingness to obey God cost him a great deal in the beginning, but because he sacrificed, God blessed him abundantly. Lot's decision, on the other hand, was selfish. He lived on the principle, "Grab the money and run. As long as I get mine, who cares?" But when God destroyed Sodom and Gomorrah, all Lot escaped with was his life. His herds, riches, his house—even his wife—were destroyed.

Where you locate your family is important to their salvation. Lot chose to live where he could find pleasure, and did not give consideration to the spiritual danger he was causing his family. He failed to see that his selfishness, which led to a prayerless, hasty, carnal choice, would lead to disaster down the road. He should have been aware of the results of his bad choice.

Not only that, but the two children produced by the incestuous relationship between Lot and his daughters were the founders of two warring tribes—the Moabites and the Ammonites—who across history remained enemies of God's people, the Israelites. Such were the results of Lot's choice to disobey God.

God had found in Abram, however, a person willing to follow Him, regardless of the cost. Such people are rare, but when God finds them, He always uses them, testing at each turn in the road to make certain the willingness to obey remains. For if a people ever start operating on the principle of selfishness, rather than the principle of obedience, they become useless to God.

If we follow Abram's life we find he was obedient. Obedience did not come easy, for Abram was a fearful man. He was always trying to negotiate a deal. In fact, on several occasions he even tried to negotiate with God. But in the long run, he always obeyed.

His biggest test of obedience came after his son, Isaac, was born. Abram, now called Abraham, was an old man. In His covenant, God had promised Abraham a son. Then came the day when God told Abraham to take his son, his only son, Isaac, and go to the mountain region known as Moriah—an isolated region where the wind moaned and howled through the wadis (dried riverbeds). There, on the top of a lonely mountain, God told Abraham to sacrifice his son as a burnt offering. Abraham never flinched. If God told him to do something, he would do it. He believed God surely would not require him to kill his son. That was not the nature of God. Yet all Abraham could do was obey—and trust God to show him something he had not yet seen.

Even as Abraham was approaching the top of the mountain to sacrifice his son, a ram was coming up the other side. And just as Abraham was getting ready to plunge the knife into Isaac's body, he heard the bleating of the ram—its horns caught in a thicket.

Then God said: "Do not lay a hand on the boy.... Now I know you fear God, because you have not withheld from

Me your son, your only son."

So Abraham sacrificed the ram instead of his son, and he called that place *Jehovah Jirah*—meaning, "the Lord will provide." When a people trust God and pray, even though they cannot see the future, they need to remember: The answer is always on the way.

Abraham's life was founded on a basic formula:

- Trust God.
- Ask God.
- Obey God.

And God never let him down.

I've discovered something about God. If you ask Him, He'll give you an answer. He is still looking for men and women who will obey Him, even when it doesn't make sense. These are the ones He is waiting to use—waiting to bless. As David said, "Trust in the Lord and He will act" (Ps 37:5).

—*Bible People Like Me*

## QUESTIONS TO CONSIDER
1. What difficult decision do you face?
2. How can you obey God in this choice?

## A PRAYERFUL RESPONSE
Lord, I will obey You, even in the tough decisions. Amen.

# DAY 12

## Going Against the Crowd

### Thought for Today

Success comes by following God instead of popular opinion.

### Wisdom from Scripture

"Now therefore revere the Lord, and serve him in sincerity and in faithfulness; put away the gods that your ancestors served beyond the River and in Egypt, and serve the Lord.

"Now if you are unwilling to serve the Lord, choose this day whom you will serve, whether the gods your ancestors served in the region beyond the River or the gods of the Amorites in whose land you are living; but as for me and my household, we will serve the Lord."

Then the people answered, "Far be it from us that we should forsake the Lord to serve other gods; for it is the Lord our God who brought us and our ancestors up from the land of Egypt, out of the house of slavery, and who did those great signs in our sight. He protected us along all the way that we went, and among all the peoples through whom we passed; and the Lord drove out before us all the peoples, the Amorites who lived in the land. Therefore we also will serve the Lord, for he is our God."

But Joshua said to the people, "You cannot serve the Lord, for he is a holy God. He is a jealous God; he will not forgive your transgressions or your sins.

"If you forsake the Lord and serve foreign gods, then he will turn and do you harm, and consume you, after having done you good."

And the people said to Joshua, "No, we will serve the Lord!"

Then Joshua said to the people, "You are witnesses against yourselves that you have chosen the Lord, to serve him." And they said, "We are witnesses."

He said, "Then put away the foreign gods that are among you, and incline your hearts to the Lord, the God of Israel."

The people said to Joshua, "The Lord our God we will serve, and him we will obey."

So Joshua made a covenant with the people that day, and made statutes and ordinances for them at Shechem.

JOSHUA 24:14-25, NRSV

## INSIGHTS FROM JAMIE BUCKINGHAM

Choices. We're all forced to make them. Shall you say no or yes? Do you give in or take a stand? Do you obey or rebel? It's tough making choices, especially when the result of your decision is unpopular—when you have to go against the crowd.

Joshua was a man who was constantly faced with choices. Most of his choices were against popular opinion. Joshua was Moses' second-in-command. Moses met him in Egypt before the Exodus began and immediately saw that Joshua was a born leader. Not only was he a leader but he understood the principle of submission. He never once coveted Moses' position. He was content to be a loyal assistant—standing with Moses when it was not the popular thing to do.

The time was twelve hundred years before Christ. The Israelites, following Moses, had miraculously escaped from Egypt where they had been slaves for many generations.

Trudging through the desert of the Sinai, they had become aware of God's love and protection. Finally, one year after leaving Egypt, they came to the border of Canaan—the Promised Land.

They camped at a place called Kadesh Barnea in the northern Sinai, just a few miles from the border of Canaan. Here they regrouped, paused to be refreshed and gained strength before taking that final step of conquest. But something happened. Moses sent twelve spies into the land of Canaan to bring back a report on the condition of the roads, the location of the cities, the morale of the people, the size of the armies, the type of agriculture and other necessary facts. He chose one man from each of the twelve tribes to do the spying. Among these was Moses' attaché—Joshua—the representative of the tribe of Ephraim.

But things did not go as Moses had planned. Instead of returning with maps and charts, the spies returned terrified. Instead of reporting on the land, they reported on the inhabitants of the land.

"The cities are huge and surrounded by insurmountable walls."

"The land is filled with giants."

Only Joshua and his friend Caleb brought back a positive report. But the negative report of the ten spies spread like infection through the crowd of Israelites.

"We're too weak," they wailed. "We're too tired. We were much better off in Egypt. We're going back. Moses is a madman and we're going to kill him." Looking at Joshua and Caleb, they said, "If you don't go along with us, we'll kill you too."

Joshua was faced with a choice. Should he stand up for what he knew was right? Should he stand up for God? Or should he go with the crowd?

Stepping before the people, he shouted, "The land we explored is a great land—flowing with milk and honey. If the Lord is pleased with us, He will take care of us. He will give us the land. But don't rebel against God. And don't be afraid of the giants—we're bigger than they are when God is on our side."

It was a tough choice. The people responded in anger and tried to stone him. He barely escaped with his life. But that night God honored Joshua's choice. He told Moses that every one of the Israelites over twenty years of age would die in the wilderness. Only Joshua and Caleb would live to take the new generation into the Promised Land.

Unbelief never sees beyond difficulties. It is always looking at walled cities and giants rather than at God. Faith looks at God; unbelief looks at obstacles. The Israelites, when they took their eyes off God, saw themselves as grasshoppers. The more they confessed their inadequacies and inabilities, the more they saw them as reality. Only Joshua and Caleb were willing to do the unpopular thing—call the people to look at God rather than the giants.

We learn from Joshua that the correct choices are not always popular. Joshua, though, had been willing to learn from Moses. Because he learned his lesson well, and because he was a man of the Bible, God promised him success. In fact, the only time the word *success* is used in Scripture is in Joshua 1:8, where God told Joshua that if he would do everything written in God's book he would be "prosperous and successful."

Success does not come by making popular decisions. It comes by obeying God.

—*Bible People Like Me*

## QUESTIONS TO CONSIDER
1. How do you define success?
2. How does your definition of success compare to God's definition?

## A PRAYERFUL RESPONSE
Lord, grant me the faith to follow You instead of the crowd. Amen.

# DAY 13

## WILLING TO OBEY

### THOUGHT FOR TODAY
God uses anyone willing to obey His commands.

### WISDOM FROM SCRIPTURE
But the scripture has imprisoned all things under the power of sin, so that what was promised through faith in Jesus Christ might be given to those who believe.

Now before faith came, we were imprisoned and guarded under the law until faith would be revealed.

Therefore the law was our disciplinarian until Christ came, so that we might be justified by faith.

But now that faith has come, we are no longer subject to a disciplinarian, for in Christ Jesus you are all children of God through faith.

As many of you as were baptized into Christ have clothed yourselves with Christ.

There is no longer Jew or Greek, there is no longer slave or free, there is no longer male and female; for all of you are one in Christ Jesus.

And if you belong to Christ, then you are Abraham's offspring, heirs according to the promise.

GALATIANS 3:22-29, NRSV

## INSIGHTS FROM JAMIE BUCKINGHAM

The most unusual and perhaps the most effective judge of Israel was a woman named Deborah. A housewife, she was gradually recognized as a woman of godly wisdom. As she grew older and her children married and left home, people began coming to her in great numbers, asking for advice and requesting that she settle their disputes. She was finally forced to set up a tent under the palm trees and actually hold court. Her natural gifts were coming to the surface.

When it became evident the Israelites could no longer tolerate the harassment of the enemy, the tribal leaders came to Deborah for help. Deborah had none of the usual qualifications given military leaders of the era. She had not trained for many years under Moses as Joshua had. She had no great physical strength like Samson. She was "just a housewife." Yet across the years she had become recognized as a woman of great wisdom.

Deborah, who was gifted as a prophet, made it clear that God was going to do something different, something the Israelites had never seen before.

Deborah prayed, knowing she would surely lose the battle unless God intervened. What did she know about military tactics? She was "only a woman." But that was her greatest asset. With a small company of soldiers, she set an ambush and exposed herself as a decoy. Knowing that the Kishon River was flooding, she and her band of Ephraimite soldiers came out on the plain, taunting the enemy. She knew Sisera was a chauvinist who disrespected women.

Deborah's taunting presence on the battlefield was more

than Sisera could take. He could not stand being challenged by an old woman and a group of poorly armed minutemen. He committed his entire army to wipe them out and roared down onto the plain with his armed chariots and soldiers wearing heavy armor.

Deborah then told her little band of troops to flee back toward the flooded stream running through the valley. Sisera pursued, and immediately his heavy chariots bogged down in the swamp. Then Deborah signaled, and Barak's army swept down from the hill and surrounded Sisera's men, driving them to the river's edge. Suddenly it began to rain. A cloudburst. Immobilized in the mud, many of the soldiers drowned in the torrential floodwaters of the river. The rest were killed by the Israelites.

Only Sisera escaped. Humiliated in defeat by an old Jewish woman, he took refuge in the tent of the only Canaanite man he knew—Heber. It was a fatal mistake. (Heber was loyal to the Israelites.) That night, after Heber's wife, Jael, had fed him supper, she waited until he was asleep. Then sneaking back into the tent, she drove a tent peg through his head with a large wooden mallet.

It was a great victory, not only for the Israelites, but for women as well, who emerged as the national heroes and were immortalized in an ancient poem called "The Song of Deborah" found in the book of Judges.

What can we learn from this? We learn that God uses whom He chooses. God is not a chauvinist, nor is He a feminist. God makes no distinction between men and women. He's simply looking for someone who is obedient, who is willing to allow his or her gifts to be used to His glory. Deborah didn't set out to be a judge, and certainly not a military leader. She just dedicated her natural abilities to God for His service.

It's easy to grow discouraged. Sometimes it seems as if life is an endless circle. But that's not necessarily so. If you do today what your hand finds to do—and do it with all your might—tomorrow might be a very significant day.

Ask Deborah!

*—Bible People Like Me*

## QUESTIONS TO CONSIDER
1. How can Deborah's story be applied to your life?
2. What can your hand find to do today?

## A PRAYERFUL RESPONSE
Lord, I am willing to begin using my untapped talents for You. Amen.

# DAY 14

## Learning to Be Courageous

### Thought for Today
One person, with God, is a majority.

### Wisdom From Scripture
Now the angel of the Lord came and sat under the oak at Ophrah, which belonged to Joash the Abiezrite, as his son Gideon was beating out wheat in the wine press, to hide it from the Midianites.

The angel of the Lord appeared to him and said to him, "The Lord is with you, you mighty warrior."

Gideon answered him, "But sir, if the Lord is with us, why then has all this happened to us? And where are all his wonderful deeds that our ancestors recounted to us, saying, 'Did not the Lord bring us up from Egypt?' But now the Lord has cast us off, and given us into the hand of Midian."

Then the Lord turned to him and said, "Go in this might of yours and deliver Israel from the hand of Midian; I hereby commission you."

He responded, "But sir, how can I deliver Israel? My clan is the weakest in Manasseh, and I am the least in my family."

The Lord said to him, "But I will be with you, and you shall strike down the Midianites, every one of them."

Then he said to him, "If now I have found favor with you, then show me a sign that it is you who speak with me.

"Do not depart from here until I come to you, and

bring out my present, and set it before you." And he said, "I will stay until you return."

So Gideon went into his house and prepared a kid, and unleavened cakes from an ephah of flour; the meat he put in a basket, and the broth he put in a pot, and brought them to him under the oak and presented them.

The angel of God said to him, "Take the meat and the unleavened cakes, and put them on this rock, and pour out the broth." And he did so.

Then the angel of the Lord reached out the tip of the staff that was in his hand, and touched the meat and the unleavened cakes; and fire sprang up from the rock and consumed the meat and the unleavened cakes; and the angel of the Lord vanished from his sight.

Then Gideon perceived that it was the angel of the Lord; and Gideon said, "Help me, Lord GOD! For I have seen the angel of the Lord face to face."

But the Lord said to him, "Peace be to you; do not fear, you shall not die."

Then Gideon built an altar there to the Lord, and called it, The Lord is peace. To this day it still stands at Ophrah, which belongs to the Abiezrites.

JUDGES 6:11-24, NRSV

## INSIGHTS FROM JAMIE BUCKINGHAM

Like most of the Israelites, Gideon was a simple farmer. He lived in the little village of Ophrah and spent his days, from dawn to dusk, toiling in the fields surrounding his village. Like all the rest, he was terrified by the Midianites. In fact, the autumn afternoon we first hear of him, he had taken his wheat and was thrashing it in a winepress behind his house.

A winepress? You don't thrash wheat in a winepress. Wheat needs to be thrashed on a big, flat rock out in the open where the wind will blow away the chaff. Not Gideon. Fearful, he was down in this hole in the ground, flailing away at his wheat with a stick because he was afraid he would be seen by the Midianites if he thrashed his wheat in the open.

Although Gideon is listed among the heroes of faith in Hebrews 11:32, it is apparent he was not a bold, dashing leader. He was simply a person like us—cautious, inhibited and a bit fearful and confused. This shows us that it's not just triumphant faith that God rewards; He rewards small faith as well.

Gideon was a harassed and discouraged man. He bore the burdens of long defeat. He had no one to stand with him and no traditions to fall back on. He had no concept of the law of Moses and knew virtually nothing of the Bible of the day. When the angel called him, he responded with bitter skepticism and a lack of understanding. He was a very unlikely man to call to lead the nation. Yet God saw something in him that he didn't even see in himself.

Some people have a lot of natural ability. Gideon didn't seem to have any. He wasn't even sure it was God calling him. Maybe this was an Amalekite dressed up like an angel. Maybe he had overdosed on wheat dust and was tripping out. He had to be sure.

He needed proof this was really God speaking. Three times he tested it, and three times God proved Himself.

Later, after Gideon had selected his small army of three hundred men according to God's instructions, he was still fearful. He could not fight the enemy by conventional means. This time, instead of waiting for Gideon to ask for another sign, God gave him one. But to receive the sign Gideon was required to do something courageous. That night God woke up Gideon and told him to take his servant, Purah, and sneak into the camp. Scared to death, Gideon did as he was told.

Kneeling outside a tent, Gideon heard a man telling about a dream he had just had. "I dreamed a round loaf of barley bread came tumbling into our camp, hit our tents and knocked them over."

"Do you know what that means?" the other soldier replied. "It means the God of the Israelites is going to use Gideon to destroy us—all of us."

Gideon rushed back to the camp, praising God all of the way.

It was a mighty victory for Gideon and his small band of soldiers. The people of Israel responded, wanting to make Gideon king. He wisely refused. "I will not rule over you, nor will my son rule over you. The Lord will rule over you" (Jgs 8:23).

What can we learn from all this?

Gideon was a person just like us—fearful and doubtful. But when he obeyed God, miracles happened.

God's ways are not our ways. We think we need a lot. God says all you need is a little—and Him. God can achieve great things with a few dedicated people who will give Him the glory. God, who looks on the heart, is able to take a person who seems to be a coward and turn him or her into a hero—as long as that person is willing to do things God's way.

—*Bible People Like Me*

## QUESTIONS TO CONSIDER

1. Is there something God wants you to do, but you're afraid to do it? If so, why?
2. How can you feel the fear and do it anyway?

## A PRAYERFUL RESPONSE

Lord, I will give my fears to You and follow Your guidance. Amen.

# DAY 15

## Learning from Mistakes

### Thought for Today

God uses and blesses people who will learn from their mistakes.

### Wisdom From Scripture

Have mercy on me, O God, according to your steadfast love; according to your abundant mercy blot out my transgressions.

Wash me thoroughly from my iniquity, and cleanse me from my sin.

For I know my transgressions, and my sin is ever before me.

Against you, you alone, have I sinned, and done what is evil in your sight, so that you are justified in your sentence and blameless when you pass judgment.

Indeed, I was born guilty, a sinner when my mother conceived me.

You desire truth in the inward being; therefore teach me wisdom in my secret heart.

Purge me with hyssop, and I shall be clean; wash me, and I shall be whiter than snow.

Let me hear joy and gladness; let the bones that you have crushed rejoice.

Hide your face from my sins, and blot out all my iniquities.

Create in me a clean heart, O God, and put a new and right spirit within me.

Do not cast me away from your presence, and do not

take your holy spirit from me.

Restore to me the joy of your salvation, and sustain in me a willing spirit.

Then I will teach transgressors your ways, and sinners will return to you.

Deliver me from bloodshed, O God, O God of my salvation, and my tongue will sing aloud of your deliverance.

O Lord, open my lips, and my mouth will declare your praise.

For you have no delight in sacrifice; if I were to give a burnt offering, you would not be pleased.

The sacrifice acceptable to God is a broken spirit; a broken and contrite heart, O God, you will not despise.

Do good to Zion in your good pleasure; rebuild the walls of Jerusalem, then you will delight in right sacrifices, in burnt offerings and whole burnt offerings; then bulls will be offered on your altar.

PSALM 51, NRSV

## INSIGHTS FROM JAMIE BUCKINGHAM

Only one man in the Bible is said to be a man after God's own heart—David.

David? Of all people? If you want to start listing the things that disqualify a person from the ministry, just list the things David did. I mean, he did them all.

- Fleeing from King Saul, David became a liar.

- Caught in his lies, David was forced to become a deceiver.

- He committed adultery with the wife of one of his army officers, got her pregnant, then had her husband killed so he could marry her.

- He was shamed before the entire nation when the prophet Nathan pointed out his sin. This caused him to have to make public confession and repentance.

- He joined the Philistines, lied to them about his intentions and then offered to betray his own people by joining the Philistines in battle against them.

- He made terrible mistakes of judgment in choosing men to stand with him, and his management policies kept the entire nation in an uproar. He seemed unable to force himself to get rid of the corrupt and ambitious leaders in his army.

- His wife ridiculed him and shamed him in public—obviously, he didn't have his home in order.

- His own children turned against him and were an embarrassment to the nation and a shame to their father.

- One son raped his own sister.

- Another son killed his brother, led a rebellion and tried to kill his father in an effort to take away his throne.

- One time David deliberately disobeyed God, went against the wishes of his advisors who knew he was disobeying God and forced the entire nation of Israel to disobey God. As a result, seventy thousand innocent people were killed.

    So David was a rebellious, disobedient leader who incited the wrath of God.

David was constantly sinning or making mistakes, then repenting, changing directions and starting over.

Yet incredibly, God said, "I have found David son of Jesse a man after my own heart; he will do everything I want him to do" (Acts 13:22).

Almost every time we read about this man in the Bible he's doing something wrong; yet God called him one of the finest—perhaps the finest—leader in all of history. How do you explain it?

I think the trait of being humble and teachable caused God to say David was a man after His own heart. He was a person like you, like me. David didn't make little mistakes—he made huge ones. And he made a lot of them. But after each mistake, after each sin, we find him repenting—and equally important, learning. His words in Psalm 51, written after repenting of another horrible sin, give us insight into the man's heart.

Despite all his flaws, David was a man after God's own heart.

God loves to use people like that—sinners who have botched up their lives but genuinely repent, admit their sin and learn from their mistakes.

*—Bible People Like Me*

## QUESTIONS TO CONSIDER
1. How can you apply God's grace to the mistakes in your life?
2. How can you become a person after God's heart?

## A PRAYERFUL RESPONSE
Lord, forgive me for my sin and renew my relationship with You. Amen.

## Yielding to God's Will

### Thought for Today

When we yield to Him, God's purposes can be accomplished.

### Wisdom From Scripture

In the sixth month the angel Gabriel was sent by God to a town in Galilee called Nazareth, to a virgin engaged to a man whose name was Joseph, of the house of David. The virgin's name was Mary.

And he came to her and said, "Greetings, favored one! The Lord is with you."

But she was much perplexed by his words and pondered what sort of greeting this might be.

The angel said to her, "Do not be afraid, Mary, for you have found favor with God.

"And now, you will conceive in your womb and bear a son, and you will name him Jesus.

"He will be great, and will be called the Son of the Most High, and the Lord God will give to him the throne of his ancestor David.

"He will reign over the house of Jacob forever, and of his kingdom there will be no end."

Mary said to the angel, "How can this be, since I am a virgin?"

The angel said to her, "The Holy Spirit will come upon you, and the power of the Most High will overshadow you; therefore the child to be born will be holy; he will be called Son of God."

LUKE 1:26-35, NRSV

## INSIGHTS FROM JAMIE BUCKINGHAM

When Elizabeth called Mary "the mother of my Lord," the young woman responded with the most beautiful and profound song ever written. We call it The Magnificat. "My soul glorifies the Lord and my spirit rejoices in God my Savior ..." (see Lk 1:46-55).

That evening, Mary probably came outside and sat under the broad expanse of the Judean stars, listening to the water flowing from the fountain and running out into the vineyards. The words of the angel echoed alive in her heart: "Do not be afraid, Mary, you have found favor with God. You will be with child.... The Holy Spirit will come upon you, and the power of the Most High will over-shadow you."

No one knows exactly where the Messiah was conceived. Gabriel's announcement to Mary was in the future tense— "You will be with child" (Lk 1:31). Elizabeth told Mary she was blessed because she believed that what the Lord had said "will be accomplished" (also future tense).

Nazareth was in the tribal area of Zebulun. To fulfill prophecy, the Messiah had to be born in Bethlehem, since it was a city of Judah. Thus the one whom the Bible called Shiloh, of the tribe of Judah, of the seed of David, had to be conceived in a city of Judah and David. This is the reason Mary left with such haste and came so quickly to Elizabeth—for it was at Ein Karem the Messiah would be conceived. It was then Mary sang her Magnificat psalm known from its first word in the Latin version, a psalm that could have come only from one who was impregnated with the Messiah.

When did it happen? That is unimportant. What is important is the attitude of this young Jewish girl—she was totally yielded to God. To be chosen by God is the greatest of all honors. Mary understood something many of us today need to learn—the more honor God puts on us, the more honor we must return to Him.

To be chosen by God has another meaning, as well. Some want to know God's will so they may weigh in advance whether to do it. God, however, reveals His will only to those who are committed to follow, whatever the cost.

Less than two miles from Ein Karem, from that little hill where Jesus' earthly life began when a humble virgin became impregnated by the Holy Sprit, stood another hill. Golgotha! There, one day thirty-three years later, Mary stood, weeping in the arms of John—one of Jesus' disciples—as men tortured and killed her son. To be chosen by God often means not only a crown of joy but a cross of sorrow. The piercing truth of God's call is this: God does not choose a person for ease and comfort and selfish joy, but for a great task that will take all he or she has to make it happen. God chooses a person to use that person. When Joan of Arc knew that her time was short, she prayed, "I shall only last a year, use me as You can."

In her heart, Mary knew there would be pain to accompany the honor. Later, after the birth of Jesus, an old prophet by the name of Simeon picked up the newborn child and looked at the mother, saying, "This child is destined to cause the falling and rising of many in Israel …

and a sword will pierce your own soul, too."

Mary knew. But she was yielded, and God used her.

*—Bible People Like Me*

## QUESTIONS TO CONSIDER
1. Have you experienced both the pain and pleasure of yielding to God? If so, how?
2. How can you stay yielded to God's will for you?

## A PRAYERFUL RESPONSE
Lord, I yield everything to You, for whatever You choose. Amen.

## LIVING WITH INTEGRITY

### THOUGHT FOR TODAY

God desires that we live with integrity.

### WISDOM FROM SCRIPTURE

In those days John the Baptist appeared in the wilderness of Judea, proclaiming, "Repent, for the kingdom of heaven has come near."

This is the one of whom the prophet Isaiah spoke when he said, "The voice of one crying out in the wilderness: 'Prepare the way of the Lord, make his paths straight.' "

Now John wore clothing of camel's hair with a leather belt around his waist, and his food was locusts and wild honey.

Then the people of Jerusalem and all Judea were going out to him, and all the region along the Jordan, and they were baptized by him in the river Jordan, confessing their sins.

But when he saw many Pharisees and Sadducees coming for baptism, he said to them, "You brood of vipers! Who warned you to flee from the wrath to come?

"Bear fruit worthy of repentance.

"Do not presume to say to yourselves, 'We have Abraham as our ancestor'; for I tell you, God is able from these stones to raise up children to Abraham.

"Even now the ax is lying at the root of the trees; every tree therefore that does not bear good fruit is cut down and thrown into the fire.

"I baptize you with water for repentance, but one who

is more powerful than I is coming after me; I am not worthy to carry his sandals. He will baptize you with the Holy Spirit and fire.

"His winnowing fork is in his hand, and he will clear his threshing floor and will gather his wheat into the granary; but the chaff he will burn with unquenchable fire."

Then Jesus came from Galilee to John at the Jordan, to be baptized by him.

John would have prevented him, saying, "I need to be baptized by you, and do you come to me?"

But Jesus answered him, "Let it be so now; for it is proper for us in this way to fulfill all righteousness." Then he consented.

And when Jesus had been baptized, just as he came up from the water, suddenly the heavens were opened to him and he saw the Spirit of God descending like a dove and alighting on him.

And a voice from heaven said, "This is my Son, the Beloved, with whom I am well pleased."

MATTHEW 3:1-17, NRSV

## INSIGHTS FROM JAMIE BUCKINGHAM

John was a person like us. A man of weakness and strength. On the one hand, he was moody, opinionated, easily discouraged. On the other hand, he was a man of great courage. He was fearless in denouncing wrong—whether he saw it among the religious and political leaders or among the common people. He called the Pharisees and Sadducees a brood of vipers; he openly denounced King Herod for marrying his brother's wife.

Yet he had a heart after God. He believed with all his heart that God had called him to prepare the people for the coming Messiah. "I baptize you with water for repentance," he said, "but after me will come One who is more powerful than I, whose sandals I am not fit to carry. He will baptize you with the Holy Spirit and with fire."

The Greek word—from which we get our word *baptism*—simply means to immerse, or plunge under. With John, water baptism was the sign that the people had been cleansed of their sin by repenting and were ready for the Messiah to appear.

While John was preaching to the crowds of people who came down to the banks of the Jordan, Jesus was taking one of the most significant steps in His life. Removing His carpenter's apron and leaving His Father's shop in Nazareth, Jesus headed south, following the road through the Jordan Valley to a public place on the river bank. Jesus had not seen John since they were boys. As youngsters they had played together during Elizabeth's brief visits. Now Jesus and John were reunited, but only briefly, as the Holy Spirit brought together these two men whose missions in life were so vastly different, yet so vitally connected.

"I've come to be baptized," Jesus said. John was weeping. "No, you should baptize me instead." Jesus was firm, but gentle. Looking John straight in the eye He said, "I am here to fulfill God's command."

It was then that John knew. Before, it had been simply a prophetic announcement. He had been speaking words he did not understand. But standing there, looking into the eyes of Jesus, he knew he was looking at the Messiah. Together they waded out into the water, and John immersed Him.

Later, while John was in prison, he began to doubt if Jesus was really the Messiah. So he sent some of his followers to question Jesus about His identity.

Jesus told the messengers to go back to John and list the miracles Jesus was performing—that would be testimony enough. He also encouraged John by saying that, even though their two ministries were vastly different, John would be blessed if he did not "fall away" because Jesus didn't meet his expectations. He then turned to the crowd that stood around Him and commended John.

John was a man like us. At times he was bold. At other times he was filled with despair. Yet in his heart he was a man of integrity. He had the courage to proclaim that Jesus was the Messiah. He also had the courage to denounce evil and injustice, knowing it would cost him his life. His mission was vastly different from the ministry of the One he came to introduce, but he was faithful. He paved the way for the Messiah and was, therefore, even though a person like us, the greatest of prophets.

*—Bible People Like Me*

## QUESTIONS TO CONSIDER
1. What does integrity mean to you?
2. How can you ensure that you're living with integrity?

## A PRAYERFUL RESPONSE
Lord, teach me how to live with integrity. Amen.

## Hearing From God

### Thought for Today
God speaks to those who will do what He tells them.

### Wisdom From Scripture
Now when Jesus came into the district of Caesarea Philippi, he asked his disciples, "Who do people say that the Son of Man is?"

And they said, "Some say John the Baptist, but others Elijah, and still others Jeremiah or one of the prophets."

He said to them, "But who do you say that I am?"

Simon Peter answered, "You are the Messiah, the Son of the living God."

And Jesus answered him, "Blessed are you, Simon son of Jonah! For flesh and blood has not revealed this to you, but my Father in heaven.

"And I tell you, you are Peter, and on this rock I will build my church, and the gates of Hades will not prevail against it.

"I will give you the keys of the kingdom of heaven, and whatever you bind on earth will be bound in heaven, and whatever you loose on earth will be loosed in heaven."

Then he sternly ordered the disciples not to tell anyone that he was the Messiah.

MATTHEW 16:13-20, NRSV

### Insights From Jamie Buckingham
Hearing God correctly is one of the major problems facing all Christians. One part of the problem is hearing

anything at all. The other part is discerning whether the voice you hear is God's or some other voice such as self, Satan or just another person's advice.

Peter was a prophet in the sense that he heard God. The first time he received "revelation knowledge" was at Caesarea Philippi. Jesus, knowing that His time on earth was drawing to a close, had asked His disciples to make the long walk with Him. Turning to His followers, He asked two world-changing questions: "Who do men say I am? Who do you say I am?"

It was at that point Simon Peter answered, "You are the Christ, the Son of the Living God."

Peter, of all people. A man like us. Yet he was the first man to receive revelation knowledge that Jesus was the Messiah. Two-and-a-half years earlier, a fisherman by the name of Andrew had introduced his brother, Simon, to Jesus. Jesus looked at Simon and told him that one day he would be called Cephas—a common Aramaic name, which means rock, or stone.

I imagine that Andrew, who felt he knew his brother far better than this young rabbi, probably chuckled. Simon will become a rock? That was the name reserved for God. "The Lord is my rock," Samuel had said (2 Sm 22:2). "Who is the Rock except our God?" David sang in the Psalms (Ps 18:31). To call anyone a rock was to equate him with God. Andrew just shook his head. This unruly, unstable, hot-tempered brother of mine whose moods change as often as the clouds cover the sun? You mean his very character will change? No way!

Simon was a chameleon who changed colors according to the environment. He had the direction and stability of a tumbleweed blown across the desert. It was impossible to believe that one day he would be so strong and solid that people would know him as Rocky. Yet that day came after Jesus ascended to heaven.

Traveling along the Mediterranean coast, Peter had stopped in Joppa, where he stayed many days with a tanner named Simon. The next morning Peter went up on the rooftop to breathe the ocean air. While Simon was fixing lunch, Peter suddenly fell into a trance and had a vision. He saw something that resembled one of the sails on a boat being let down from heaven by four corners. In it were all kinds of animals and reptiles and birds. "This is your lunch, Peter," a voice said.

"Not me, Lord," Peter answered. "I'm Jewish. I must obey the dietary laws. None of those things are kosher. They're all unclean." Instantly the voice replied, "Do not call anything unclean that God has made clean."

While Peter was standing there scratching his head, there was a knock at the door below. The visitors were messengers from a Roman centurion named Cornelius who lived up the coast in the other Caesarea. A believer in Christ, although a gentile, he had been visited by an angel the day before. The angel told him to send men down to Joppa, that Peter could be found there. Cornelius was to gather all his gentile friends and have Peter preach to them.

"While Peter [was preaching], the Holy Spirit came on all who heard the message. The circumcised believers who had come with Peter were astonished that the gift of the Holy Spirit had been poured out even on the gentiles. For they heard them speaking in tongues and praising God" (Acts 10:44-46).

Peter immediately ordered a baptism service. There was

no way he could deny what God was doing. Just as God had shown him that Jesus was the Messiah, so He showed him on the rooftop at Joppa, and in the house of Cornelius, that all people—Jews, Gentiles, Blacks, Whites, Asians, Hispanics, men, women—all are welcome in the kingdom of God. No one is unclean.

Because Peter was willing to hear God, the gospel was not confined to the Jews alone, but now belonged to the entire world. Because Peter heard God and acted on what he heard, the Holy Spirit is still building the church, and men and women everywhere are receiving revelation knowledge that Jesus is the Christ, the Son of the Living God.

*—Bible People Like Me*

## Questions to Consider
1. How do you know when God is speaking to you?
2. What would you like to hear from Him today?

## A Prayerful Response
Lord, speak, for Your servant is listening and willing to obey. Amen.

# TRAVELING THE WILDERNESS

The wrong that pains my soul below
    I dare not throne above,
I know not of His hate,—I know
    His goodness and His love.

I dimly guess from blessings known
    Of greater out of sight,
And, with the chastened Psalmist, own
    His judgments too are right.

JOHN GREENLEAF WHITTIER,
FROM "THE ETERNAL GOODNESS"

See, I am doing a new thing!
Now it springs up; do you not perceive it?
I am making a way in the desert
and streams in the wasteland.

ISAIAH 43:19, NIV

## JAMIE BUCKINGHAM'S INSIGHT

The purpose of the wilderness is to lead us to God's healing fountains.

# DAY 19

## WILDERNESS HOSPITALITY

### THOUGHT FOR TODAY
In the wilderness God sends messengers to comfort us.

### WISDOM FROM SCRIPTURE
One day, after Moses had grown up, he went out to where his own people were and watched them at their hard labor. He saw an Egyptian beating a Hebrew, one of his own people.

Glancing this way and that and seeing no one, he killed the Egyptian and hid him in the sand.

The next day he went out and saw two Hebrews fighting. He asked the one in the wrong, "Why are you hitting your fellow Hebrew?"

The man said, "Who made you ruler and judge over us? Are you thinking of killing me as you killed the Egyptian?" Then Moses was afraid and thought, "What I did must have become known."

When Pharaoh heard of this, he tried to kill Moses, but Moses fled from Pharaoh and went to live in Midian, where he sat down by a well.

Now a priest of Midian had seven daughters, and they came to draw water and fill the troughs to water their father's flock.

Some shepherds came along and drove them away, but Moses got up and came to their rescue and watered their flock.

When the girls returned to Jethro their father, he asked

them, "Why have you returned so early today?"

They answered, "An Egyptian rescued us from the shepherds. He even drew water for us and watered the flock."

"And where is he?" he asked his daughters. "Why did you leave him? Invite him to have something to eat."

Moses agreed to stay with the man, who gave his daughter Zipporah to Moses in marriage.

Zipporah gave birth to a son, and Moses named him Gershom, saying, "I have become an alien in a foreign land."

EXODUS 2:11-22, NIV

## INSIGHTS FROM JAMIE BUCKINGHAM

The first reaction to the wilderness is withdrawal. The pain of losing a loved one, the shock of losing a job, the deep disappointment of being betrayed by someone you love—all tend to drive us into deep withdrawal.

Invariably, our first reaction is, "Leave me alone."

God understands this. He also understands our even greater need to be part of a family—to be touched by loving hands, held by loving arms. Thus, into every wilderness experience of ours, God sends special messengers to minister to us. To Jesus He sent angels. To Elijah He sent ravens. To Moses He sent an old Bedouin sheikh.

Jethro, with warm, simple hospitality, helped the former prince of Egypt emerge from his shell of grief and self-pity and enter a world of preparation, a world designed by God to train him for the time he would return to Egypt for a far greater purpose.

Moses, at age forty, had been second-in-command in the most powerful and academically advanced nation in history.

As an infant, he had been rescued from the sword of Pharaoh and raised by Pharaoh's daughter as a prince. Trained in courtly manners and given the best education available, his foster mother looked for the day when Moses would replace her father on the throne of Egypt.

But God had other plans, plans that could come to pass only after the egotism of Egypt had been burned from His servant in the crucible of the wilderness.

Formal education is only the beginning of spiritual preparation. At the age of forty, Moses entered God's graduate school. The next forty years were spent in the deprivation of the wilderness. These were years in which his rough edges were sanded smooth. The literal blast of the furnace of the Sinai refined the character of a man God was going to use. There he learned to pray and learned the value of solitude. There, sitting with a few sheep and goats, he learned the principles of leadership. But he did not have to struggle alone. God put a family around him—the family of Jethro—who taught him the ways of the desert people, the ways of hospitality.

This unwritten code of hospitality is still practiced in the Sinai. It is a code that originated with Abraham, whom Jew and Moslem both call the "Father of Hospitality." It was Abraham who first decreed that the essentials of life were never to be denied any wilderness pilgrim, be he friend or enemy.

Desert hospitality captures this truth: There are some things that belong to God, and thus belong to all people. It is the lesson of hospitality—the lesson of sharing.

It would have been natural for Moses to have withdrawn into a shell of self-pity when he left Egypt. But, as the psalmist reminds us, God sets the solitary in families (see Ps 68:6). Such families are not like prisons, with wardens constantly checking and requiring. Families are freeing institutions, opening the doors and windows of the jails into which we withdraw when we are alone.

To Moses God gave the family of Jethro. Intellectual reasoning, even preaching, were not enough to set Moses free from the bondage of grief and isolation. God knew Moses did not need preachments. He needed love. What he needed was what we all need—an arm around his shoulder, a soft bosom on which to lay his head, a good meal, fellowship in a family and a gentle voice saying, "I understand." Beyond that man cannot go, but God stands at the door beckoning.

In our wilderness wanderings we will eventually learn that. We will learn to diminish our preaching, refrain from advice and directions and follow the example of Jethro: "Why did you leave him alone? Invite him to have something to eat."

Of such is the kingdom of heaven. It is a free gift, a gift we shall one day replenish when we pass this way again.

—*A Way Through the Wilderness*

## QUESTIONS TO CONSIDER
1. Are you passing through the wilderness? If so, what does it feel like?
2. How can you partake of God's hospitality in this barren place?

## A PRAYERFUL RESPONSE
Lord, thank You for Your hospitality in the wilderness. Amen.

# DAY 20

## God's Call

### Thought for Today
God still calls us by name to accomplish specific tasks.

### Wisdom from Scripture
Now Moses was tending the flock of Jethro his father-in-law, the priest of Midian, and he led the flock to the far side of the desert and came to Horeb, the mountain of God.

There the angel of the Lord appeared to him in flames of fire from within a bush. Moses saw that though the bush was on fire it did not burn up.

So Moses thought, "I will go over and see this strange sight—why the bush does not burn up."

When the Lord saw that he had gone over to look, God called to him from within the bush, "Moses! Moses!" And Moses said, "Here I am."

"Do not come any closer," God said. "Take off your sandals, for the place where you are standing is holy ground."

Then he said, "I am the God of your father, the God of Abraham, the God of Isaac and the God of Jacob." At this, Moses hid his face, because he was afraid to look at God.

The Lord said, "I have indeed seen the misery of my people in Egypt. I have heard them crying out because of their slave drivers, and I am concerned about their suffering.

"So I have come down to rescue them from the hand

of the Egyptians and to bring them up out of that land into a good and spacious land, a land flowing with milk and honey—the home of the Canaanites, Hittites, Amorites, Perizzites, Hivites and Jebusites.

"And now the cry of the Israelites has reached me, and I have seen the way the Egyptians are oppressing them.

"So now, go. I am sending you to Pharaoh to bring my people the Israelites out of Egypt."

But Moses said to God, "Who am I, that I should go to Pharaoh and bring the Israelites out of Egypt?"

And God said, "I will be with you. And this will be the sign to you that it is I who have sent you: When you have brought the people out of Egypt, you will worship God on this mountain."

Moses said to God, "Suppose I go to the Israelites and say to them, 'The God of your fathers has sent me to you,' and they ask me, 'What is his name?' Then what shall I tell them?"

God said to Moses, "I AM WHO I AM. This is what you are to say to the Israelites: 'I AM has sent me to you.' "

God also said to Moses, "Say to the Israelites, 'The Lord, the God of your fathers—the God of Abraham, the God of Isaac and the God of Jacob—has sent me to you.' This is my name forever, the name by which I am to be remembered from generation to generation."

EXODUS 3:1-15, NIV

## INSIGHTS FROM JAMIE BUCKINGHAM

The tragedy of our wilderness experience is not that we have to go through grief and suffering, but that we often miss the blessings from burning bushes—the things through which God speaks. Through a letter from a friend, the words of a book, a long-forgotten song, the voice of a teacher, the beauty of a holy life, the innocence of a child, God still calls us by name and makes His eternal purpose known.

Even then, though we may see the miraculous and hear in the midst of it a voice calling our name, nothing is fulfilled until we respond. The Scriptures are full of stories of divine summons and the people who responded—people like Moses who had been prepared and were now ready to be used.

Learning to wait patiently, learning to do today what your hand finds to do, learning to hear the call of God when it comes, and to respond—that is what the wilderness is all about. Once a man or woman submits his or her life to God's control, he or she voluntarily surrenders the right to determine or the power to vary the consequences of that decision. From that moment on, no situation can ever come into the life of the believer that has not first passed through the hands of God, and thus has redeeming quality.

Our task, even though we may be wandering in some wilderness, is to remain ready. Our lamps should never be allowed to run low on oil, for who knows when a summons may come? Blessed is the free, unengaged spirit who has not encumbered himself or herself with the things and cares of this world, who can at once put aside all he is doing to answer the call of God.

Many years later the prophet Isaiah would encourage a battered people to wait upon the Lord. Waiting, Isaiah said, would bring renewed strength. While the word *wait* in Hebrew has several connotations, the word used in Isaiah 40 means "to be entwined about, to become part of." It is best illustrated by looking at a braided rope that is actually several strands woven together to become one large, strong strand. Though the smaller ropes are actually separate, they become one because they have been entwined and twisted together.

Moses had spent forty years waiting. But the waiting was not limited to the passing of time. It had to do with faithful service to Jethro—and the task before him. He had learned that service to God often meant nothing more than doing with all his might what his hand found to do.

Waiting on the Lord, as one does in a wilderness experience, means we should become entwined with Him, braided into Him, as we become part of Him and He becomes part of us.

The burning bush gave direction to Moses' life—a life that for eighty years had been spent in preparation. He had been called by God, handed a commission and sent forth to accomplish a task.

To all those wandering in the wilderness, let it be said: Bushes still catch on fire and God still calls people by their names. But the call comes only to those who are busy with the smaller tasks already assigned.

—*A Way Through the Wilderness*

## QUESTIONS TO CONSIDER
1. What are you waiting to receive from God?
2. What task can you accomplish in the meantime?

## A PRAYERFUL RESPONSE
Lord, I will wait until I hear You call my name. Amen.

# DAY 21

## HIDDEN PROMISES

### THOUGHT FOR TODAY
When we obey God, we benefit from His promises.

### WISDOM FROM SCRIPTURE
When Pharaoh's horses, chariots and horsemen went into the sea, the Lord brought the waters of the sea back over them, but the Israelites walked through the sea on dry ground.

Then Miriam the prophetess, Aaron's sister, took a tambourine in her hand, and all the women followed her, with tambourines and dancing.

Miriam sang to them: "Sing to the Lord, for he is highly exalted. The horse and its rider he has hurled into the sea."

Then Moses led Israel from the Red Sea and they went into the Desert of Shur. For three days they traveled in the desert without finding water.

When they came to Marah, they could not drink its water because it was bitter. (That is why the place is called Marah.)

So the people grumbled against Moses, saying, "What are we to drink?"

Then Moses cried out to the Lord, and the Lord showed him a piece of wood. He threw it into the water, and the water became sweet. There the Lord made a decree and a law for them, and there he tested them.

He said, "If you listen carefully to the voice of the Lord your God and do what is right in his eyes, if you pay attention to his commands and keep all his decrees, I will not bring on you any of the diseases I brought on the Egyptians, for I am the Lord, who heals you."

EXODUS 15:19-26, NIV

## INSIGHTS FROM JAMIE BUCKINGHAM

God never brings a hindrance into our lives that He does not intend to be used to open another door that would not have opened otherwise.

When God spoke to Moses at the burning bush at the base of Mt. Sinai, commissioning him to return to Egypt to lead the Israelites out of bondage, He had a clear-cut plan. He said He was concerned about the suffering of the Israelites. He said He had to come to rescue them and to take care of them as they traveled, and that He would bring them to Mt. Sinai to worship Him (see Ex 3:7-12).

But such promises are hard to remember when you run out of water in the desert.

In Exodus 15:25, the historical account says the Lord was testing the people at Marah. In the Western concept, testing is for the purpose of ascertaining knowledge. It is used to determine how much one has learned. But the biblical concept of testing is not to ascertain knowledge; it is a method of teaching. When God "tests" His people, He is not doing so to find out whether they have learned their lesson and deserve a good grade. God's tests are learning experiences, designed by the Teacher to share knowledge, not to determine its presence or absence.

Thus, when God tested the people at Marah, He did it with a decree, not a questionnaire. It is a marvelous promise that, like all God's promises, is conditional—found in the subjunctive mood and preceded by an *if*. The promise of the absence of disease is for those who (1) listen carefully to the voice of the Lord; (2) do what is right in His eyes; (3) pay attention to His commands; and (4) keep all His decrees. Only then does a person have the right to claim the promise of "none of these diseases."

An old Bible teacher used to remind his pupils that not only was the Lord interested in getting the people out of Egypt, He also wanted to get Egypt out of the people. That, perhaps, is at the heart of all wilderness experiences. In this case, the people brought a lot of Egypt with them—internally. Now at Marah, the Lord spoke and told them He would not allow the Egyptian disease to afflict them—if they but obeyed Him.

What did God want the Israelites to do? Obviously, He wanted them to drink the water of Marah. But it was filled with magnesium. True, but even Moses could not have known about the medicinal qualities of calcium and magnesium. For one thing, magnesium is a powerful laxative. It was God's way of cleaning out their systems. Had they drunk the bitter water, and continued to drink it despite its effects on their intestines, their bodies would have ceased the purgative action and grown accustomed to the water. In the process, however, they would have expelled most of the amoebae, parasites and death-dealing germs they brought with them from Egypt.

There is another medicinal quality about the water of Marah. Calcium and magnesium form the basis of a drug called *dolomite*. Dolomite pills are used by professional athletes who perform in the sun. It is basically a muscle control drug to be used in extremely hot weather [to control spasms].

Over and over we are reminded that the reason for wilderness experiences is purification and preparation. The water of Marah would have certainly brought almost instant purification. God was about to change the entire eating structure of the nation. No longer would they gorge themselves on shellfish, pork and the highly spiced foods of Egypt. To accomplish this change, God started with a purge, ridding the Israelites of all their perverse yearnings and desires. He was about to introduce them to their new dietary structure known ever since as "kosher." But the people rebelled at the first test. Thus the promise of a people without diseases had to wait for a generation who listened carefully to the voice of the Lord and did not grumble at His commands.

The principle holds true even today. God wants us not only to live, but to live abundantly. His desire is for us to have long, productive and creative lives. So He continually leads us back to the water of Marah where our crusty spirits may be broken, and the Spirit of God may enter.

*—A Way Through the Wilderness*

## QUESTIONS TO CONSIDER
1. Has God asked you to obey Him in a specific situation? Explain.
2. What could be a hidden promise in this act of obedience?

## A PRAYERFUL RESPONSE
Lord, I will respect and obey Your personal guidance to me. Amen.

## LIVING WATERS

### THOUGHT FOR TODAY

Only God can quench our inner thirst.

### WISDOM FROM SCRIPTURE

But he [Jesus] had to go through Samaria.

So he came to a Samaritan city called Sychar, near the plot of ground that Jacob had given to his son Joseph.

Jacob's well was there, and Jesus, tired out by his journey, was sitting by the well. It was about noon.

A Samaritan woman came to draw water, and Jesus said to her, "Give me a drink."

(His disciples had gone to the city to buy food.)

The Samaritan woman said to him, "How is it that you, a Jew, ask a drink of me, a woman of Samaria?" (Jews do not share things in common with Samaritans.)

Jesus answered her, "If you knew the gift of God, and who it is that is saying to you, 'Give me a drink,' you would have asked him, and he would have given you living water."

The woman said to him, "Sir, you have no bucket, and the well is deep. Where do you get that living water?

"Are you greater than our ancestor Jacob, who gave us the well, and with his sons and his flocks drank from it?"

Jesus said to her, "Everyone who drinks of this water will be thirsty again, but those who drink of the water that I will give them will never be thirsty. The water that I will give will become in them a spring of water gushing up to eternal life."

The woman said to him, "Sir, give me this water, so that I may never be thirsty or have to keep coming here to draw water."

JOHN 4:4-15, NRSV

## INSIGHTS FROM JAMIE BUCKINGHAM

Spiritual thirst, the need for living water, is the dominating factor in the lives of all human beings. It begins with a deep longing for something to satisfy inner cravings. Although we realize Jesus said the person who hungers and thirsts after righteousness will be filled (Matthew 5:6), we are often shocked to find we are thirsting for the wrong things. We don't want righteousness; we prefer selfish gain and pleasure. The desire pursues us from Egypt and tracks us across the deserts of our lives, until we cry out as Paul did: "When I want to do good, evil is right there with me.... . What a wretched man I am! Who will rescue me from this body of death?" (Rom 7:21-24).

In fact, it is these very cravings that cause many of us to behave in such a way that we are forced into the wilderness to begin with.

In his concept of the God-shaped vacuum, St. Augustine once prayed, "Our hearts are restless until we find our rest in Thee." Thus, while it is thirst that drives us forward, we are never satisfied, no matter how much we drink, until we drink from the fountain of Living Water.

It is not enough, in the desert, to depend on surface water—blessings that fall intermittently. Humanity needs a much deeper source of life than that brought by showers of blessings. People must have a source upon which they can draw when there has been no rain for years.

David wrote about the spiritual person who was "like a

tree planted by streams of water, which yields its fruit in season" (Ps 1:3). Interestingly, the Spanish Bible does not translate "streams" with the usual Spanish word *rio*. It uses the less common word *arroyo*. The river David was talking about was not a flowing stream but a dry gulch—a wadi. The spiritual person does not need constantly flowing water in order to prosper. He or she prospers even when the skies are cloudless and the land is parched. He or she prospers because his or her roots, on the upstream side of the dike, go deep into the sand and draw from the underground supply.

Cisterns are not adequate when the sun grows hot and there is no rain for years. Jeremiah warned the people of Israel about the danger of this. "My people have committed two sins," the Lord said through Jeremiah. "They have forsaken me, the spring of living water, and have dug their own cisterns, broken cisterns that cannot hold water" (Jer 2:13).

Neither cisterns nor wells give a sure supply of water. Only the presence of a spring, where water flows freely of its own accord, affords certainty. Elim (where the Israelites stopped to drink in the wilderness) was such a place, with twelve springs surrounded by numerous date palms. This water was not collected by man's efforts, nor did it have to be drawn to the surface by man's efforts. It flowed freely for anyone who could come and drink.

Jesus was talking about this when he sat at Jacob's well in Samaria. In the story in John 4, He was sitting on the edge of a well when a Samaritan woman approached to draw water. In His conversation with her, Jesus said, "Everyone who drinks this water will be thirsty again, but whoever drinks the water I give him will never thirst. Indeed, the water I give him will become in him a spring of water welling up to eternal life" (Jn 4:13-14).

The King James Version says, "A well of water springing up." But that is a poor translation. Jesus never talks about wells; He talks of springs. A well is something people have to dig. A spring is a gift from God. Religious people—Pharisees and others who feel they have to earn salvation—dig wells. The spring, like God's grace, bubbles up from underground of its own accord. You don't have to do anything to earn it. You don't have to labor for it. Like salvation, it is a free gift to all who stoop to drink.

At another time Jesus spoke more of this: "If anyone is thirsty, let him come to me and drink. Whoever believes in me, as the Scripture has said, *streams* of living water will flow from within him" (Jn 7:37, italics added).

The writers say Jesus was speaking of the Holy Spirit who is never a cistern, never a well, but always a spring. He becomes a river flowing out of the heart of all those who come to Jesus and drink of Living Water.

The wilderness prepares us to become more than a vessel to hold water. In the wilderness we actually become a source of water for others.

For every Marah, there is an Elim just beyond. We are never bidden by God in our wilderness trek to continue to drink the bitter water. After the crucifixion comes the glorious resurrection. At Elim we rest. We encamp near the water. Here He makes His sheep lie down in green pastures and leads us beside the still waters. Here our souls are restored.

What a God is ours! He drowns our foes in the sea and disciplines His children in the next breath. He leads us to the bitter waters of Marah, then urges us to move on to the cool shade of Elim. He thunders from the mountaintop but feeds

His flock and gently leads those that are with young. In every desert there is an Elim. Here we pause, are refreshed and move on to a land of streams and rivers.

—*A Way Through the Wilderness*

## QUESTIONS TO CONSIDER
1. For what does your soul thirst? Where are you trying to quench this thirst?
2. How could God fill this thirst for you?

## A PRAYERFUL RESPONSE
Lord, quench my spiritual thirst with Your refreshing Spirit. Amen.

# DAY 23

## Changed Appetites

### Thought for Today
God disciplines us to change our worldly appetites.

### Wisdom From Scripture
Now when the people complained in the hearing of the Lord about their misfortunes, the Lord heard it and his anger was kindled. Then the fire of the Lord burned against them, and consumed some outlying parts of the camp.

But the people cried out to Moses; and Moses prayed to the Lord, and the fire abated.

So that place was called Taberah, because the fire of the Lord burned against them.

The rabble among them had a strong craving; and the Israelites also wept again, and said, "If only we had meat to eat!

"We remember the fish we used to eat in Egypt for nothing, the cucumbers, the melons, the leeks, the onions, and the garlic; but now our strength is dried up, and there is nothing at all but this manna to look at."

Now the manna was like coriander seed, and its color was like the color of gum resin.

The people went around and gathered it, ground it in mills or beat it in mortars, then boiled it in pots and made cakes of it; and the taste of it was like the taste of cakes baked with oil.

When the dew fell on the camp in the night, the manna would fall with it.

NUMBERS 11:1-9, NRSV

## INSIGHTS FROM JAMIE BUCKINGHAM

God has a keen ear. It is especially tuned to those caught in desert experiences, for God does not allow His children to experience the wilderness without purpose. Even the changing of our diet from meat to manna is part of God's greater plan for our lives.

God has a purpose for everything He does. There was purpose in the manna. Granted, manna was not what they ordered off God's menu. They wanted the food of Egypt. Yet God's ways are not our ways. His provision often looks superficial to the carnal mind. "If we are God's 'chosen people,' why do we have such a meager diet? We should eat like kings—like the pharaoh."

It was the sin of presumption, for they felt they knew better than God what they should eat. They were too shortsighted to understand a God who insisted on closing the door to Egypt's food forever, and who was more interested in teaching them the discipline of obedience than in satisfying their carnal cravings.

When Moses refused to listen to their grumbling and requests to turn back, they rebelled. It was, in essence, a counterrevolution—a common problem faced by all revolutionary leaders whose followers, after their first victories, often grow discouraged over the sparse diet and long trek before reaching the Promised Land.

God prescribed a strict diet of manna along with restrictions for gathering and storing. It was more than many could take. It's not that they wanted to return to bondage; they just wanted a quick respite into the past—an overnight excursion, so to speak, back to sin.

But such excursions are always forbidden by God, for they bring with them a rekindling of old tastes for things not healthy. Manna was not tasty. But God was changing tastes. He was transforming a group of sloppy, undisciplined former slaves into an army. There is no place for gourmet menus in the wilderness. Here people exist on bare essentials—getting their minds off their bellies and onto God.

The manna of God was to be only temporary. Just a few days ahead lay the Promised Land with milk, wine and honey. Only further disobedience caused God to have to keep the manna coming—for forty years.

The carnal appetite, which God was burning from them with His prescribed diet, is never satisfied. It always yearns for more. It causes people to run after every new "prophet" who comes on the scene with a "new revelation" from God. It causes them to trade the written Word of God for the philosophy of the world, since it seems more palatable. It causes people to demand melons and meat while disdaining what God has placed before them.

But the only way to reach the Promised Land is by eating God's diet. Leeks, onions and garlic will not get you into Canaan, for that diet is always accompanied by the bondage of Egypt. In the wilderness we must make priority decisions. Are we willing to give up what satisfies the belly to have what satisfies the soul?

Those who ignore or refuse God's provision while lusting for the former things (which the Bible says must eventually be "put away") will soon perish and be burned in the sands of the wilderness—the very place where God's manna, which they rejected, covered the earth.

Yet the others—those who accept God's meager diet on faith, believing God has a purpose for what He serves up—

enter into a marvelous truth that lean diets are intended only for a season. To those who obey and do not grumble, there lies ahead a table in the wilderness. Here, then, is the truth: While we are in the wilderness, we *are not of* the wilderness. We are bound for the Promised Land.

*—A Way Through the Wilderness*

## QUESTIONS TO CONSIDER
1. What appetites hinder your walk with God?
2. How can you allow God to change them?

## A PRAYERFUL RESPONSE
Lord, please exchange my worldly appetites for Your desires. Amen.

# DAY 24

## WILDERNESS PILGRIMS

### THOUGHT FOR TODAY
God keeps His people on the move.

### WISDOM FROM SCRIPTURE
"Thus says the Lord, your Redeemer, the Holy One of Israel: For your sake I will send to Babylon and break down all the bars, and the shouting of the Chaldeans will be turned to lamentation.

"I am the Lord, your Holy One, the Creator of Israel, your King.

"Thus says the Lord, who makes a way in the sea, a path in the mighty waters, who brings out chariot and horse, army and warrior; they lie down, they cannot rise, they are extinguished, quenched like a wick: Do not remember the former things, or consider the things of old.

"I am about to do a new thing; now it springs forth, do you not perceive it? I will make a way in the wilderness and rivers in the desert.

"The wild animals will honor me, the jackals and the ostriches; for I give water in the wilderness, rivers in the desert, to give drink to my chosen people, the people whom I formed for myself so that they might declare my praise."

ISAIAH 43:14-21, NRSV

## Insights From Jamie Buckingham

There are three kinds of people in the wilderness. The hermits move in from the outside, settle in caves and stay in one place until they die. The Bedouin are nomads, on the move but always in a circle. However, God never intends for His children to settle in the wilderness as hermits or nomads. We are thus to be the third breed of wilderness person—the pilgrim. Each wilderness experience becomes a pilgrimage—an experience in which we meet, know and follow God to His land of promise.

The process is simple, although often painful.

The chemist, the Holy Spirit, takes the elements of our lives and drops them into the mortar of the wilderness setting. Then, using circumstances as a pestle, He crushes our natural elements until they come into union with each other. Pouring that fine dust into a crucible, He turns up the heat until all the impurities burst into tiny flames and disappear, leaving behind the purified self, perfectly integrated, ready for service—working all things together for good.

This is never a static process. It always involves change and progress from one stage to another. It can be done only on the move.

To some degree, all life on earth is a wilderness experience. As surely as sparks fly upward, Job pointed out, we are born into trouble. But the wilderness is a passage through trouble, not a place to stop and wallow in our adversity. As the old Negro spiritual says, "This world is not my home, I'm just a-passin' through."

Every road sign on our trek through the wilderness of this mortal life points toward a glorious consummation of life eternal with God. We are not born to die; we are born to be reborn and live forever. As we move toward that heavenly experience, which waits all the saints, we pass through trouble, adversity, grief, pain and hardships—all wilderness experiences. But these deserts are not designed to choke the life from us; rather, they are designed to mold us and shape us into the image of Christ. We are not ever to allow ourselves to become desert settlers like the hermits of old, or even the Bedouin of today. We are pilgrims, "a-passin' through."

Life is designed by God as a pilgrimage composed of many wildernesses. God is forever saying to all of us, "Travel light." Do not stop to build monuments. Do not overload yourself with sentimental memorabilia that ties the heartstrings to things of the past. Do not stake your sections of land as "sacred" and declare you can never leave them behind. If you have precious belongings, send them ahead. For as Jesus said, "Where your treasure is, there your heart will be also" (Mt 6:21).

I still shudder when I recall the half-sneer, half-laugh from the Jewish archaeologist when I asked about Jewish shrines. "We Jews do not build shrines," she said. "Only Christians stop to do that. We worship a God who is on the move."

It is one of the important lessons of the desert: Keep moving! The pilgrim who pauses too long in any one place dies. Even the Bedouin, who seem bound like Prometheus to the rock of their wilderness wanderings, realize they must keep on the move. The Bedouin, though, are not pilgrims. They are nomads, wandering with the seasons in circles, with no Promised Land to beckon them onward. They are the prototype of spiritual squatters who camp smugly at a certain point of tradition or doctrine—while the winds of God's Spirit blow past.

There is the story of hermits who fled to the Sinai during the fourth and fifth centuries. Monks, recluses, they moved out of the mainstream of life and never returned. Mistakenly, they thought the cloud had come to rest over them permanently.

Their pilgrimage, as they saw it, was inner. They came to stay in order to take an inward journey to personal salvation. But in the process they stagnated. Instead of becoming servants, they became dependent upon others more practical and utilitarian to serve them. Eventually—like the Dead Sea which receives but never gives—some became mad parasites and died. And while a few did indeed come face-to-face with God, most hermits remain tragic examples in history of pilgrims who view the clouds as stationary.

We must learn a lesson from the hermits, though it be a negative one. We are never called to enter a wilderness to find God, which is the essence of religion. Rather, when circumstances force us into the wilderness, we should have faith to believe God will take the initiative and reveal Himself to us in His time and place. Our responsibility is to respond, and stay under the cloud as it moves to God's destined purpose for our lives.

To view the wilderness as an end—a place of abiding, rather than a place through which one passes on his way to a land of promise—is the greatest of tragedies. Since God never intended that His children enter a wilderness and remain, each wilderness experience should be accompanied by a sense of nagging dissatisfaction, a deep longing for the Promised Land to come. Pilgrims should be careful not to try to escape the suffering God places on His children, until the object of that suffering is complete. At the same time, they should arise every morning and look upward—expecting, yea knowing, that one day the cloud will move.

—*A Way Through the Wilderness*

## QUESTIONS TO CONSIDER
1. Do you sense God is moving you in a new direction? If so, describe it.
2. What could keep you from following God in this way?

## A PRAYERFUL RESPONSE
Lord, help me to remove the barriers to moving on with You. Amen.

---

## THE POWER OF PATIENCE

### THOUGHT FOR TODAY

God takes His time to accomplish His will.

### WISDOM FROM SCRIPTURE

Happy are those who do not follow the advice of the wicked, or take the path that sinners tread, or sit in the seat of scoffers; but their delight is in the law of the LORD, and on his law they meditate day and night.

They are like trees planted by streams of water, which yield their fruit in its season, and their leaves do not wither. In all that they do, they prosper.

The wicked are not so, but are like chaff that the wind drives away.

Therefore the wicked will not stand in the judgment, nor sinners in the congregation of the righteous; for the Lord watches over the way of the righteous, but the way of the wicked will perish.

PSALM 1, NRSV

### INSIGHTS FROM JAMIE BUCKINGHAM

Some things cannot be learned on the run. They must be learned slowly. They must be walked out through the experience of time.

It is difficult to hear God on the run. Elijah discovered this truth many years after Moses learned the same thing. Not until the prophet got quiet and waited on the high oasis on the mountain was he able to hear.

So it is with all impatient men, for God is not seen by

those in rapid transit. Isaiah heard only after he pulled aside from the throng of worshipers in the temple and sat quietly in the presence of God. David heard Him on the hillside tending his lambs, alone with harp and flute. Jesus heard best when He withdrew from the mobs—even from His disciples—and took time to spend the night praying on some mountain, or kneeling alone in a garden. John the apostle, with nothing but the time of exile on his hands, heard Him as he waited patiently on the isle of Patmos.

The soft occasions do not bring out the deepest of a person. Only as we sink roots into the hard, rocky soil of the wilderness, only as we wait patiently for the bush to burn, only as we withdraw for our own forty days and forty nights of waiting, do we find the Source. The trouble, it seems, is that God is not in a hurry, and we are.

One of the great virtues learned in the wilderness is patience. In the desert you forget calendars. You leave your watch behind, for it is useless. You go to bed at sunset and rise at dawn. Meals are scheduled by body needs, not to satisfy clocks and appointments. In the desert, one learns to wait.

How programmed we are to produce! Goal-oriented, production-conscious, we have been trained to close each day with a question: How much did I produce today? Did I meet my quota? Everything is geared to what the production control people call "the bottom line"—which is preceded invariably by a dollar sign. It is a mentality developed by a materialistic society that places the prime emphasis on doing rather than being.

But in the wilderness, you learn patience. Here you have time—lots of it. There is time to grow still. Time to pull aside and look at a bush burn. Time to sit with friends and talk. Time to pray. Time to explore. Time to rest. Time to walk long distances without the anxiety of having to be back to meet a schedule. In the desert you rediscover the precious commodity of time. As faith has been boxed in by religious rites, so has time been relegated by our hurry-up society into a framework of calendars and clocks. Only in the wilderness do you discover how precious it is to have enough time to do what you want.

God may be found in the wilderness. But the entire scale of time and place in the wilderness is "utterly other," apart from time and space as we know it in our rapid-transit society.

In my times in the desert I have become aware of its age-lessness and vastness. Each time I have entered the Sinai I have purposefully taken off my watch and left my appointment calendar behind. Here it makes no difference how old I am, what the date is or whether it is 9:00 A.M. or noon. I have learned to get up with the dawn and crawl into my sleeping bag when the sun sets.

Desert trees do not bloom on command. The date palm, for instance, produces its fruit in its season. Then it waits patiently as the next crop is prepared. No amount of commands to "Hurry up!" will make it produce faster. It waits on God's time.

The psalmist said the blessed man is "like a tree planted by streams of water, which yields its fruit in season and whose leaf does not wither" (Ps 1:3).

There are seasons when the man of God flourishes spiritually. Then there are times when the leaves of our life fall, the fruit disappears and for all appearances the tree is lifeless. But each tree has a season, and in the proper season the fruit reappears.

I have walked through the agriculture experimentation station in Israel where these industrious people have developed trees that produce fruit all year long. These trees have fruit and blossoms on their branches at the same time. But the fruit is never as tasty as that which comes from the tree that produces only once a year, then waits patiently for the next crop to mature.

The psalmist equates the "blessed man" with a tree "planted by streams of water." It is a strange simile when you consider the wilderness, for there are no such rivers in the desert. The best you find is dry riverbed, a wadi, which is filled with water only on occasion.

The difference is profound. Any tree can produce when planted on the shores of a sparkling river. But in the wilderness, where there are no rivers, the fruit trees need to find nourishment in another way. The beautiful date palm for instance, which produces the most delicious of all desert fruit, finds water by sending its roots into the underground reservoirs. It does not depend on showers of blessings to keep it producing, but draws its strength from the hidden nourishment found deep in the soil of the wilderness.

This is the lesson of the desert. When your branches are barren, when all your buds have dried up, when you have drooped in discouragement, remember your roots. Remember that just beneath the sand there are underground reservoirs where the water is pure. Relax. Take your time. And know that in your season, you shall eat fruit again.

—*A Way Through the Wilderness*

## Questions to Consider
1. For what do you feel anxious today?
2. How can you "wait upon the Lord" in this situation?

## A Prayerful Response
Lord, while I wait, I will sink my roots deeply in You. Amen.

# DAY 26

## The Way of Intercession

### Thought for Today
God hears our urgent intercession for those in need.

### Wisdom From Scripture
Then Moses turned and went down from the mountain, carrying the two tablets of the covenant in his hands, tablets that were written on both sides, written on the front and on the back.

The tablets were the work of God, and the writing was the writing of God, engraved upon the tablets.

When Joshua heard the noise of the people as they shouted, he said to Moses, "There is a noise of war in the camp."

But he said, "It is not the sound made by victors, or the sound made by losers; it is the sound of revelers that I hear."

As soon as he came near the camp and saw the calf and the dancing, Moses' anger burned hot, and he threw the tablets from his hands and broke them at the foot of the mountain.

He took the calf that they had made, burned it with fire, ground it to powder, scattered it on the water, and made the Israelites drink it.

Moses said to Aaron, "What did this people do to you that you have brought so great a sin upon them?"

When Moses saw that the people were running wild (for Aaron had let them run wild, to the derision of their enemies), then Moses stood in the gate of the camp, and said, "Who is on the Lord's side? Come to me!" And all the sons of Levi gathered around him.

He said to them, "Thus says the Lord, the God of Israel, 'Put your sword on your side, each of you! Go back and forth from gate to gate throughout the camp, and each of you kill your brother, your friend, and your neighbor.'"

The sons of Levi did as Moses commanded, and about three thousand of the people fell on that day.

Moses said, "Today you have ordained yourselves for the service of the Lord, each one at the cost of a son or a brother, and so have brought a blessing on yourselves this day."

On the next day Moses said to the people, "You have sinned a great sin. But now I will go up to the Lord; perhaps I can make atonement for your sin."

So Moses returned to the Lord and said, "Alas, this people has sinned a great sin; they have made for themselves gods of gold.

"But now, if you will only forgive their sin—but if not, blot me out of the book that you have written."

EXODUS 32:15-21, 25-32, NRSV

## INSIGHTS FROM JAMIE BUCKINGHAM

During the March from Egypt to Mount Sinai, God primarily spoke to Moses. Only on rare occasions, such as at the springs of Marah, did the people hear His voice. The rest of the time He was reflected in the pillar of cloud by day and the column of fire at night—the God of no name and no image.

The revelation of the Law on Mount Sinai had a great impact, since now the God of history, the God of underived existence, made Himself known. Bit by bit, in the process known as progressive revelation, God revealed Himself—first to Moses and then to the people.

In the biblical account of the meetings between God and Moses on Mt. Sinai, a marvelous progress of familiarity begins to take place. It begins with the formal statement in Exodus 19:3: "Then Moses went up to God, and the LORD called to him from the mountain."

Following this, Moses descended to the plain to report to the people. Twice more he ascended the mountain, each time coming back to warn the people of God's holiness.

What happened on the mountain that last trip has no comparison in history save what happened many years later at Calvary. Confessing the sin of his people, Moses took the place of the lonely advocate between God and the people. He was convinced of God's justice and did not see how God could go back on His solemn threat to destroy the nation. Yet if that judgment were to be averted, it must be in consequence of an atonement. The only thing he could offer was himself. *Yet,* he wondered, *was that enough?*

Someplace along the line, during his conversations with God, Moses had come to understand that God was not only a God of justice, He was a God of mercy. And even though words like *lovingkindness* and *our Father* were yet to be defined, Moses had learned through his wilderness wanderings that only by suffering could one redeem another. It was the law of substitution. In deep pathos, therefore, the prince and leader of the nation fell on his face before God and proposed that he, the chosen servant, should be weighed in the scale against the people and that God should accept his blood as a ransom for their life.

"Oh, what a great sin these people have committed! They have made themselves gods of gold. But now, please forgive their sin—" His words faltered. He could speak no more; this supreme gesture on his part was choked by a paroxysm of grief, a sob of irrepressible emotion.

Finally the words came forth: "But if not, then blot me out of the book you have written" (Ex 32:31-32).

Years later Jesus would remind His followers that this concept of self-sacrifice reflects the very heart of God's purpose for the world. "Greater love has no one than this, that he lay down his life for his friends" (Jn 15:13).

Moses had learned the ultimate lesson of the wilderness— that the love of God will cause us to give ourselves fully and completely for others.

*—A Way Through the Wilderness*

## QUESTIONS TO CONSIDER

1. Is there someone for whom you wish to intercede?
2. What will you pray for this person?

## A PRAYERFUL RESPONSE

Lord, forgive Your people for their sins. Amen.

## GOD'S SILENCE

### THOUGHT FOR TODAY

In silence, we find God's presence.

### WISDOM FROM SCRIPTURE

Moses said to the Lord, "See, you have said to me, 'Bring up this people'; but you have not let me know whom you will send with me. Yet you have said, 'I know you by name, and you have also found favor in my sight.'

"Now if I have found favor in your sight, show me your ways, so that I may know you and find favor in your sight. Consider too that this nation is your people."

He said, "My presence will go with you, and I will give you rest."

And he said to him, "If your presence will not go, do not carry us up from here.

"For how shall it be known that I have found favor in your sight, I and your people, unless you go with us? In this way, we shall be distinct, I and your people, from every people on the face of the earth."

The Lord said to Moses, "I will do the very thing that you have asked; for you have found favor in my sight, and I know you by name."

Moses said, "Show me your glory, I pray."

And he said, "I will make all my goodness pass before you, and will proclaim before you the name, 'The Lord'; and I will be gracious to whom I will be gracious, and will show mercy on whom I will show mercy.

"But," he said, "you cannot see my face; for no one shall see me and live."

And the Lord continued, "See, there is a place by me where you shall stand on the rock; and while my glory passes by I will put you in a cleft of the rock, and I will cover you with my hand until I have passed by; then I will take away my hand, and you shall see my back; but my face shall not be seen."

EXODUS 33:12-23, NRSV

## INSIGHTS FROM JAMIE BUCKINGHAM

The most awesome aspect of the desert, perhaps the most terrifying aspect, is its total silence.

No place on earth is as silent as the Sinai. To those of us surrounded by noise, who have grown accustomed to the "madding crowd," the silence of the desert quickly becomes a fearsome thing.

For most people, silence creates a nervousness, an anxiety that forces us to seek noise; and if we do not find it, to create it. To some, silence becomes a gaping abyss that swallows us up, forcing us to turn inward to the even more awesome wilderness of self-understanding and self-revelation. To others, silence is the playground of our demons, which we keep fenced in only by our much talking and much activity. To grow silent opens the gates. Thus we fear the silence and go to great lengths to escape it.

But the desert is silent. Here there are no insects, no chirping katydids, no croaking frogs. Even the wind is silent as it blows noiselessly across the barren sand. The silence is so loud it is frightening. Yet it is here, in the silence, that God speaks loudest.

Silence is often equated—or at least linked in our minds—

with darkness. Yet men of wisdom have learned, as Moses did on Mt. Sinai, that God dwells in the darkness. When God called Moses to the summit of the mountain to receive the Law, the entire mountain was covered with a thick cloud. As Moses ascended, he disappeared from sight to the people watching from below. The cloud grew darker until he was in total darkness. Yet there he found God. This was later confirmed by the shepherd king, David, who discovered that even the darkness is not dark to God. Indeed, "the night will shine like the day, for darkness is as light to you" (Ps 139:12).

Perhaps this cannot be fully understood unless you, too, have walked in the darkness of the wilderness. Surely it is one of the great purposes of our wilderness experience to teach us the value of total silence—to train us to listen to the still, small voice of God and to feel His presence in the darkness. Here in the wilderness, we discover that even the valley of the shadow of death holds no fear, "for thou art with me."

Moses returned from his encounter with God a man of few words. Yet something had happened inside him. His face literally glowed with the glory of God—a shine that was so great he had to actually wear a veil to keep from being conspicuous. The words he did speak, however, were words of great power.

Words rooted in the soil of God are words that have emerged from the silence and lead us back into the silence.

Silence, we have been told, is emptiness. But in our walk through the wilderness, as we close our door on the shouts of men, the clashing of ideas, the clamor of things, even the music of praise, we find that silence is not emptiness but Fullness and Presence. Here we get a glimpse of the great mystery of God—the mystery of God's own speaking.

Out of the silence and darkness of the past, God spoke the Word and through His Word created heaven and earth. As it was in the past, so it shall be in the future. For when the final seal—the seventh seal—was broken in John's revelation of things to come, there was silence in heaven for about half an hour. Only when the silence was complete, and God's awesome mystery fully comprehended, was the angel allowed to approach the golden altar before the throne with the spoken prayer of the saints. Only after the silence were the seven angels allowed, one at a time, to put the trumpets to their lips to sound the blast that heralded the advent of the establishment of God's eternal kingdom. Words may be the instruments of this present world, but silence is the mystery of the future world, and heralds the presence of God (see Rev 8).

There is a time, it seems, in our walk through the wilderness, that we must risk walking in darkness and silence. It is at this time we must take our understanding and comprehension of things as they seem, fold it into our backpack and walk with only the hand of God guiding us.

That is the lesson of the silence in the wilderness.

—*A Way Through the Wilderness*

## Questions to Consider
1. How do you feel about extended silence?
2. How might you find God in the silence?

## A Prayerful Response
Lord, manifest Your presence in the silence. Amen.

## THROUGH THE SOLITUDE

### THOUGHT FOR TODAY

Solitude with God prepares us for living.

### WISDOM FROM SCRIPTURE

The same night he [Jacob] got up and took his two wives, his two maids, and his eleven children, and crossed the ford of the Jabbok.

He took them and sent them across the stream, and likewise everything that he had.

Jacob was left alone; and a man wrestled with him until daybreak.

When the man saw that he did not prevail against Jacob, he struck him on the hip socket; and Jacob's hip was put out of joint as he wrestled with him.

Then he said, "Let me go, for the day is breaking." But Jacob said, "I will not let you go, unless you bless me."

So he said to him, "What is your name?" And he said, "Jacob."

Then the man said, "You shall no longer be called Jacob, but Israel, for you have striven with God and with humans, and have prevailed."

Then Jacob asked him, "Please tell me your name?" But he said, "Why is it that you ask my name?" And there he blessed him.

So Jacob called the place Peniel, saying, "For I have seen God face to face, and yet my life is preserved."

The sun rose upon him as he passed Penuel, limping because of his hip.

GENESIS 32:22-31, NRSV

## INSIGHTS FROM JAMIE BUCKINGHAM

There are times when a person needs family and friends to comfort, affirm, correct or heal. But there are other times when each of us needs to be alone, totally withdrawn from all human voice or presence, separated from the world in solitude with God.

Whereas silence is passive, solitude is an act of seeking and finding that place of aloneness. Deep inside, all of us seem to know intuitively that until we withdraw from all we consider necessary to our comfort, we will not come face-to-face with God. It is that nagging truth that keeps driving me back into the desert. It is that same truth that has sustained me as I have walked through my own inner wilderness.

Only in times and places of solitude do people have genuine confrontation. Jacob was a family man, surrounded by wives, concubines, children, kinsmen, handmaids, warriors and workers. But there came a time in his life when he realized he could no longer hide from himself. Sending everyone ahead, he knelt one night beside the Brook Jabbok and entered into solitude. There ensued that night a great battle as Jacob wrestled with a heavenly being. As dawn approached and it was evident Jacob's stubbornness had not yielded, the angel started to leave. But Jacob, realizing he was fighting against something he desperately needed, cried out, "I will not let you go unless you bless me" (Gn 32:26).

The blessing came in the form of a hip deformity. From that time on, Isaac's younger son walked with a limp. But his life, as well as his name, was changed. No longer was he called *Jacob*, the manipulator. Now he was called *Israel*—one who wrestled with God, and lost.

When our wrestling is alone, as with Jacob at the Brook Jabbok, we come to understand the real battles we face are not with others but with self—and with God. Only then do we understand that the purpose of the wilderness is not to break us but to soften us as we may be molded into the image of God's Son. For God does not want broken people, only people who are yielded.

Moses, Elijah, David and Jesus—and millions of others who have walked through the wilderness—discovered that solitude is not a curse but a blessing. It is not something to be feared but a treat to be desired.

Thomas Merton, who spent the last years of his life as a hermit, said his contemplative solitude brought him into intimate contact with others. In his diary he wrote: "It is in deep solitude that I find the gentleness with which I can truly love my brothers. The more solitary I am, the more affection I have for them. It is pure affection and filled with reverence for the solitude of others."

Merton, of course, was right. It needs to be mentioned, however, that while solitude brings us into an encounter with God, the lack of conflict with brothers and sisters, the absence of "rubbing," often presents a false image of true love—a love without confrontation.

Solitude, however, does not separate us from those we truly love, but brings us instead into deep communion with them—even though we may not see them for long periods of time. It teaches us to respect the solitude of others. We do not go crashing in every time we see someone alone, feeling that we must provide company, for we realize that to do so might interrupt the deepest communion one can have—communion with God and with self.

There is a vast difference, of course, between solitude and loneliness. While loneliness is inner emptiness, solitude is inner fulfillment. As loneliness is not healed by companionship, however, neither does solitude become beneficial simply because one is alone. The lonely person has no inner time or inner rest to wait and listen. He wants answers to his overpowering questions, solutions to his constant problems. But in true solitude, we learn we can be alone and not lonely. In solitude we come face-to-face with the One who satisfies all our needs. It's not that He necessarily answers all of our questions or solves all our problems. But when we are alone with Him, they just don't seem important anymore.

So we enter solitude, as Moses entered the darkness of the Mountain of God, with no other motive than to be alone with the Father. We do not enter in order to return and share what we have learned. If we do this, we will spend our solitude time taking notes on how to apply truth to the lives of others. No, we enter solitude as an end in itself, not as a means to share the experience with others.

We enter solitude to see the face of God, to commune with Him as friend to friend, to let Him speak to us about the deep things in our hearts, and with an utter contentment to remain in solitude forever if He so wills. It is only then that God sends us back down the mountain to the people below who are struggling with the concept of community, to teach them that only as we come into His presence do we understand the true meaning of living in the presence of others.

—*A Way Through the Wilderness*

## QUESTIONS TO CONSIDER

1. How could you create times of solitude with God?

2. What would you expect from this solitude?

## A PRAYERFUL RESPONSE

Lord, help me to find solitude with You. Amen.

## SPIRITUAL SETBACKS

### THOUGHT FOR TODAY

Even in the Promised Land, we need God's help to manage opposition.

### WISDOM FROM SCRIPTURE

O Lord, you have searched me and known me.

You know when I sit down and when I rise up; you discern my thoughts from far away.

You search out my path and my lying down, and are acquainted with all my ways.

Even before a word is on my tongue, O Lord, you know it completely.

You hem me in, behind and before, and lay your hand upon me.

Such knowledge is too wonderful for me; it is so high that I cannot attain it.

Where can I go from your spirit? Or where can I flee from your presence?

If I ascend to heaven, you are there; if I make my bed in Sheol, you are there.

If I take the wings of the morning and settle at the farthest limits of the sea, even there your hand shall lead me, and your right hand shall hold me fast.

If I say, "Surely the darkness shall cover me, and the light around me become night," even the darkness is not dark to you; the night is as bright as the day, for darkness is as light to you.

O that you would kill the wicked, O God, and that the bloodthirsty would depart from me—those who speak of you maliciously, and lift themselves up against you for evil!

Do I not hate those who hate you, O Lord? And do I not loathe those who rise up against you?

I hate them with perfect hatred; I count them my enemies.

Search me, O God, and know my heart; test me and know my thoughts.

See if there is any wicked way in me, and lead me in the way everlasting.

PSALM 139:1-12, 19-24, NRSV

## INSIGHTS FROM JAMIE BUCKINGHAM

Why do those of us who live in the Promised Land keep finding ourselves back in the wilderness?

Surely, it seems, having once tasted the blessings of God, there should be no desire, no need, ever to return to the wilderness wanderings. Is not our ultimate goal to enter Canaan? Once there, then, why do we continually find ourselves back in the desert—wandering, thirsting, discouraged and sometimes without hope?

Part of the confusion may stem from our misunderstanding of the nature of the Promised Land. The wilderness, in many aspects, was an easier place to live than the Promised Land. Granted, it was a place of wandering, a place of hard teaching, a place of painful purification. But it was also a place of provision and protection. There was free food every morning. There was protection from the vipers. God was visible through the day and night in the pillar of cloud and the pillar of fire. There was never any doubt about which direction to move. Concerning their entire forty-year trek, God reminded the Israelites, "Your clothes did not wear out, nor did the sandals on your feet" (Dt 29:5).

Yet when the wilderness training was over and the people of God entered the Promised Land, everything changed.

God's plan for His people in the Promised Land is far greater than the extinction of all desires. In the Promised Land, desire and passion are heightened. Granted, that necessitates self-control. But God never takes away our desires and passions. Instead, He heightens them. Then He focuses them to be used and enjoyed inside the framework He has designed. Sexual pleasure is designed for culmination in marriage. The desire and consumption of fine food and wine is to be enjoyed inside the framework of self-control. In the wilderness every step was directed by the finger of God, but in the Promised Land, while men and women are free from the bondage of legalistic law, they are now governed by laws written on the heart. Such laws, I might add, demand far more discipline than those chiseled in stone.

Even though God promised Joshua all the land where he set his foot, it was still up to the people actually to "possess" the land. That was accomplished not by sitting and waiting, but by aggressive military campaigns. In the Promised Land the opposition was fierce. The cities (which had been promised the Israelites) were walled and occupied by giants. The fields (which had been prepared) not only had to be tilled, planted, weeded and harvested, but the farmers constantly had to fight off invading bands of marauders who waited until the crops were ready and then swept down to plunder and steal.

It is not easy living in the Promised Land. In fact, to some degree it is simpler and easier to live in the wilderness—an argument brought up many times by those who wanted to return to the bondage of Egypt, and again by those who voted at Kadesh-Barnea not to go in and occupy the land.

So why do people constantly find themselves returning to the wilderness? Perhaps the place of adversity is not the wilderness at all. Perhaps we have grown so accustomed to God's provision for wilderness people, we do not recognize that the hardships being encountered are unique to those who live in the Promised Land.

Despair, temptation, discouragement, conflict—these are not just wilderness situations. These are situations faced by those in the Promised Land as well. Training and growth continue even after we enter the Promised Land—and perhaps in heaven as well.

In God's Promised Land, even though there is conflict and pain, struggle and despair, it is for the purpose of growth and change. Instead of absorbing our spirits into His Spirit, He heightens our individuality by placing His Spirit within each of us. Thus we begin to experience the ultimate of being—individuality. With individuality comes the anxiety of having to make decisions and the pain of suffering the consequence of wrong decisions. God never intended man to become senseless. Rather, He intends us to use all our senses, to become in the highest degree sensual people. Such is the promise of the Promised Land.

*—A Way Through the Wilderness*

## QUESTIONS TO CONSIDER
1. What do you expect from reaching your Promised Land?
2. What opposition might you meet there? How can you prepare for it?

## A PRAYERFUL RESPONSE
Lord, thank You for being with me in the Promised Land. Amen.

## COVENANT LOVE

### THOUGHT FOR TODAY

God's covenant love never forsakes us.

### WISDOM FROM SCRIPTURE

But the whole congregation threatened to stone them. Then the glory of the Lord appeared at the tent of meeting to all the Israelites.

And the Lord said to Moses, "How long will this people despise me? And how long will they refuse to believe in me, in spite of all the signs that I have done among them?

"I will strike them with pestilence and disinherit them, and I will make of you a nation greater and mightier than they."

But Moses said to the Lord, "Then the Egyptians will hear of it, for in your might you brought up this people from among them, and they will tell the inhabitants of this land. They have heard that you, O Lord, are in the midst of this people; for you, O Lord, are seen face to face, and your cloud stands over them and you go in front of them, in a pillar of cloud by day and in a pillar of fire by night.

"Now if you kill this people all at one time, then the nations who have heard about you will say, 'It is because the Lord was not able to bring this people into the land he swore to give them that he has slaughtered them in the wilderness.'

"And now, therefore, let the power of the Lord be

great in the way that you promised when you spoke, saying, 'The Lord is slow to anger, and abounding in steadfast love, forgiving iniquity and transgression, but by no means clearing the guilty, visiting the iniquity of the parents upon the children to the third and the fourth generation.' Forgive the iniquity of this people according to the greatness of your steadfast love, just as you have pardoned this people, from Egypt even until now."

Then the Lord said, "I do forgive, just as you have asked; nevertheless—as I live, and as all the earth shall be filled with the glory of the Lord—none of the people who have seen my glory and the signs that I did in Egypt and in the wilderness, and yet have tested me these ten times and have not obeyed my voice, shall see the land that I swore to give to their ancestors; none of those who despised me shall see it.

"But my servant Caleb, because he has a different spirit and has followed me wholeheartedly, I will bring into the land into which he went, and his descendants shall possess it.

"Now, since the Amalekites and the Canaanites live in the valleys, turn tomorrow and set out for the wilderness by the way to the Red Sea."

NUMBERS 14:10-25, NRSV

## INSIGHTS FROM JAMIE BUCKINGHAM

There are certain times in every person's life when he or she makes decisions that change the entire course of destiny. These are "hinge moments" on which swings the future. This was such a time in the life of Moses. God was offering him the inheritance He had promised earlier to Abraham. No longer would Moses have to contend with the fainthearted, the unfaithful, the grumblers, the unbelievers. In a single moment God would wipe out the entire nation of unbelievers and start afresh with Moses and those faithful men who stood with him.

"Accept it," said the spirit of self. "You've gone the second mile. You've turned the other cheek. This opportunity will never come again. Take your rest and enjoy all that is due you."

"No," said Moses' nobler self. "At stake is far more than my own self. As much as I yearn to rest, to no longer have to fight with these squabbling people, to become a second Abraham, I cannot do it. I have made vows to these people, and even if they do not want my love, I have no choice but to love them. If they cannot inherit the land, then I cannot do it either. Such is the price of covenant love."

Just ahead, only a few miles to the north, were the mountains of the Promised Land—a land flowing with milk and honey. It was all his, with God's blessings. He was within a day's march of paradise. It was the fruition of his life. All he had to do was turn his back on those who were refusing his love and move ahead. He glanced up at the mob surrounding him, some still holding the stones they would have used to kill him. There they were, standing like marble statues, immobilized by the mighty presence of the glory of God, their expressions frozen on their faces, unable to speak or move.

Were they worth giving up all he had earned over these forty years in the wilderness? Were they worth dying for? Across the years perhaps there echoed a word that would one day redeem not just the nation of Israel but the entire earth: "But God demonstrates his own love for us in this: While we were still sinners, Christ died for us" (Rom 5:8, NIV).

"I cannot accept the offer," Moses whispered into the dust where he lay on his face before God. "I cannot go over and possess the land because they cannot go with me."

Moses knew the moment he uttered the statement what God's verdict would be: "Turn back tomorrow and set out toward the desert." In his spirit he knew his decision would mean he would never see the Promised Land. But he had no choice, if he were to remain true to his character. He could not take the rest he longed for at the expense of the people to whom he had committed himself, even though they had disowned him. So he turned away from the open gate to paradise and chose to suffer with the people in their affliction, rather than enjoy the pleasures of Canaan without them.

It was a rugged path he chose to walk, a path that would mean another forty years in the wilderness and a lonely death on Mount Nebo, still just out of reach of the Promised Land. But it was a decision that saved the nation of Israel and softened God's heart so that despite His heavy judgment, a remnant was saved to go in at a later time to take what God had promised.

So Moses chose the road of covenant love, the lonely road. In doing so he chose the road that God's Son, many years later, would walk also—a road that, despite the pain of having to see His servant suffer on behalf of His people, brought immense pleasure to God.

—*A Way Through the Wilderness*

## QUESTIONS TO CONSIDER
1. How has God's covenant love been faithful to you?
2. How can you express covenant love to someone in your life?

## A PRAYERFUL RESPONSE
Lord, thank You for Your covenant love toward me. Amen.

# BELIEVING FOR MIRACLES

Once to every man and nation
    comes the moment to decide;
In the strife of Truth with Falsehood,
    for the good or evil side;
Some great cause, God's new Messiah,
    offering each the bloom or blight,
Parts the goats upon the left hand and sheep upon the
    right,
And the choice goes by forever twixt that darkness
    and the light.

JAMES RUSSELL LOWELL, "THE PRESENT CRISIS"


"The Spirit of the Lord is on me, because he has anointed me to preach good news to the poor. He has sent me to proclaim freedom for the prisoners and recovery of sight for the blind, to release the oppressed, to proclaim the year of the Lord's favor."

LUKE 4:18-19, NIV

## JAMIE BUCKINGHAM'S INSIGHT

For those who will believe, the miracles of the Bible are still miracles for today.

# DAY 31

## NOTHING BUT THE BEST

### THOUGHT FOR TODAY
God makes miracles out of the ordinary.

### WISDOM FROM SCRIPTURE
On the third day a wedding took place at Cana in Galilee. Jesus' mother was there, and Jesus and his disciples had also been invited to the wedding.

When the wine was gone, Jesus' mother said to him, "They have no more wine."

"Dear woman, why do you involve me?" Jesus replied. "My time has not yet come."

His mother said to the servants, "Do whatever he tells you."

Nearby stood six stone water jars, the kind used by the Jews for ceremonial washing, each holding from twenty to thirty gallons.

Jesus said to the servants, "Fill the jars with water"; so they filled them to the brim.

Then he told them, "Now draw some out and take it to the master of the banquet." They did so, and the master of the banquet tasted the water that had been turned into wine. He did not realize where it had come from, though the servants who had drawn the water knew. Then he called the bridegroom aside and said, "Everyone brings out the choice wine first and then the cheaper wine after the guests have had too much to drink; but you have saved the best till now."

This, the first of his miraculous signs, Jesus performed at Cana in Galilee. He thus revealed his glory, and his disciples put their faith in him.

JOHN 2:1-11, NIV

## INSIGHTS FROM JAMIE BUCKINGHAM

The purpose for all miracles is to glorify God. Miracles have no other purpose. All miracles come from God and are designed so God gets the glory and the credit. God does not want people to get the credit or the glory. He is displeased when men or women allow themselves to be called miracle workers. He doesn't want churches to say they are miracle-working churches. When that sort of thing happens, God takes the power away and gives it to those who give Him all the glory. God will not share His glory with any other.

Jesus knew that, which is probably one of the reasons He began His public miracle ministry in such an unobtrusive manner.

The master of the banquet tasted the water that had been turned into wine, not realizing where it had come from. He called the bridegroom aside and said, "Everyone brings out the choice wine first and then the cheaper wine. But you have saved the best till now."

That which was transformed was better than that which was manufactured. This is one of the vast incomprehensibles about God. The things of God are always better than the things of man. Everything we make with our hands is secondary to that which God makes and transforms.

It is meaningful that Jesus chose an ordinary ceremony— a wedding—to perform His first miracle. God always uses the ordinary. When the angel came to Mary to tell her she had conceived, he met her—not in the temple—but in a private place. When it was time for the Son of God to be born, He was birthed in a stable. It was shepherds who received the first angelic visit. The Son of God spent His early years in a carpenter's shop.

God is a God of the ordinary. How appropriate that the first miracle would be at the wedding of a nameless village peasant who was suffering the embarrassment of having run out of wine. Jesus wanted us to know that not only does God enjoy celebrations, He is a God of the ordinary. Miracles are not reserved for heads of state, missionaries and television preachers, they are for us. They take place in impossible situations—when the wine runs out—to teach us that humanity's extremity is God's opportunity, and that delays of mercy are not to be construed as denials of prayer.

Jesus never put restrictions on miracles. He never said, "If you will become a Christian, then God will give you a miracle." Miracles, He indicates, are for everyone— believer and nonbeliever alike. The wine was for all. But there were those at the wedding who were "called." They had chosen to follow Jesus. They were the greatest benefi- ciaries. Most just enjoyed the wine and went about their merriment. But those who knew Jesus had changed the water into wine did more—they became believers in a mir- acle-working God. Years later, they, too, enjoyed the same power that Jesus had.

The marvelous part of God's grace is how He pours it out on everybody. The rain falls on the just and the unjust. It doesn't just fall on the crops of the Christians. It falls on both sides of the road. When God pours out His grace, He pours it out on all of us.

Many of us have never seen water turned into wine. But a

number of people have experienced God's miraculous provision. On several occasions, a poor woman in our church in Florida discovered the food in her refrigerator was being restored, day by day. She would go to bed at night with only a few swallows of milk left in the milk carton—not enough to give to her child the next day. Awaking in the morning, she would find the carton almost filled.

More important, she testified, was the new joy of God put in her heart day after day—the kind of joy a bride feels at a wedding.

The evidences remain. Whenever Jesus comes into a life, there is a new quality. What He does is sparkling. His new wine is never flat. It bubbles. It's spumante. Exciting. Exhilarating. Thrilling. The life that Jesus brings is rich and full—nothing but the best as He takes the water of our lives and turns it into wine.

*—Miracle Power*

## QUESTIONS TO CONSIDER
1. What "ordinary" miracle do you need from God?
2. What everyday miracles has He performed for you in the past?

## A PRAYERFUL RESPONSE
Lord, grant me the faith to ask You for miracles. Amen.

# DAY 32

## Power Over Nature

### Thought for Today

Because Christ resides in us, we have dominion over this world.

### Wisdom From Scripture

That day when evening came, he said to his disciples, "Let us go over to the other side."

Leaving the crowd behind, they took him along, just as he was, in the boat. There were also other boats with him.

A furious squall came up, and the waves broke over the boat, so that it was nearly swamped.

Jesus was in the stern, sleeping on a cushion. The disciples woke him and said to him, "Teacher, don't you care if we drown?"

He got up, rebuked the wind and said to the waves, "Quiet! Be still!" Then the wind died down and it was completely calm.

He said to his disciples, "Why are you so afraid? Do you still have no faith?"

They were terrified and asked each other, "Who is this? Even the wind and the waves obey him!"

MARK 4:35-41, NIV

### Insights From Jamie Buckingham

"Who is this man?" the disciples ask. "Even the wind and the waves obey Him."

Jesus said what He had just done was done by "faith." He indicated that the disciples could have done the same thing if they had faith.

There are basically two kinds of miracles. There are those miracles that happen because God Himself intervenes. No prayer, no faith, no human agent is involved. God simply overrides a law of nature because He sees what needs to take place and there is no person to do it.

Other miracles involve a person. In these, a person is the agent God uses to bring the miracles to pass. When a person gets involved, faith becomes a major factor. What is faith? Faith is simply believing God is in charge and has given to us all the dominion He gave to Jesus.

We have dominion over the things of this world because Christ is in us. Jesus was, and is, the Living God. When He comes into us in the person of His Holy Spirit, He brings with Him all His power and authority. To the Colossian Christians Paul pointed out that Christ is the hope of glory (see Col 1:27). He went ahead to say, "You have been given fullness in Christ, who is the head over every power and authority" (Col 2:10). In short, all the power and dominion of Jesus resides in us.

What is the power and dominion that resides in Jesus?

The night before He was crucified Jesus told His disciples, "I tell you the truth, anyone who has faith in Me will do what I have been doing" (Jn 14:12). What had He been doing? He had been healing the sick, casting out demons and taking authority over nature. He went on to further challenge His followers by saying, "He (those who believe in Jesus) will do even greater things than these, because I am going to the Father. And I will do whatever you ask in My name, so that the Son may bring glory to the Father. You may ask Me for anything in my name, and I will do it" (Jn 14:12-14).

Followers across the centuries have been confused by the meaning of "the name of Jesus." When Jesus tells us to pray in His name, He is not referring to the closing words of a prayer that ends, "In Jesus' name, amen." He is talking about recognizing Him for who He is, His power, His dominion. The little formula, "In the name of Jesus" is meaningless unless we recognize who He is, that He is in us.

It is Jesus' dominion over all things—including nature—that gave Him authority to stand up in the boat and say to nature, "I'm going to override you. I am in charge here. You, natural law, you wind and waves, hear Me! Your boss, your Creator is speaking! I'm telling you to change, to stop this, to be calm, to sit down and to shut up." He says it to demons, and He says it to the sea. Both obey Him.

When something happens to me, when the wind blows across my lake and there are waves in my life, I go find a little kid to pray for me. I don't want someone praying for me who is filled with worldly knowledge. I want someone who believes, someone who is willing to claim the power of Jesus as a given and walk it out. That's the reason Jesus said if you want to enter the kingdom of heaven, you will have to come as a little child.

That's not to say that we should get rid of all worldly knowledge. It simply means we should not lean on our own understanding.

When Jesus stood and rebuked the waves, all He did was exert His natural being—that which has been promised in prophecy and which was intended for all believers. "But at your rebuke the waters fled, at the sound of your thunder they took to flight" (Ps 104:7). Although in his psalm David was talking about the creation process—the creation power—the power of the Creator over nature remained evident in God's Son. Now, His natural being was also supernatural, because He was not tainted by sin as we are tainted by sin. For us to have this same power we, as adults, must go through a process. Jesus was born—and remained—sinless. By that the Bible means he never doubted nor disobeyed God. Therefore, when He was faced with a situation that was hindering the will of God, it was natural for him to take authority. Jesus was living in dominion.

It was never for His own benefit. He never changed a camel into a Cadillac. He never even changed the rocks into bread so He could have something to eat. The night He was arrested He could have called the angels (who were at His beck and call) to protect Him from the soldiers. Instead, He submitted Himself to God's higher plan—the plan of the cross. He never profited a single time.

Now the big question is this: Is this kind of miracle for today, or are we simply at the mercy of those who report the weather without having authority over the weather?

The idea that we have authority over the weather is foreign to us. But let's pause and consider: God did not set certain laws of the universe in motion, then step back out of the way. Rather, He has given us the same authority He gave Jesus to override these laws—when it is His will—so that His higher purpose may be accomplished.

*—Miracle Power*

## QUESTIONS TO CONSIDER

1. What can you learn from the story of Jesus calming the sea?
2. Do you agree that we have dominion over nature? Why, or why not?

## A PRAYERFUL RESPONSE

Lord, teach me to live in the power of Your name. Amen.

# DAY 33

## Power Over Demons

### Thought for Today
Even demons flee in the presence of Jesus.

### Wisdom From Scripture
They went across the lake to the region of the Gerasenes.

When Jesus got out of the boat, a man with an evil spirit came from the tombs to meet him.

This man lived in the tombs, and no one could bind him any more, not even with a chain.

For he had often been chained hand and foot, but he tore the chains apart and broke the irons on his feet. No one was strong enough to subdue him.

Night and day among the tombs and in the hills he would cry out and cut himself with stones.

When he saw Jesus from a distance, he ran and fell on his knees in front of him.

He shouted at the top of his voice, "What do you want with me, Jesus, Son of the Most High God? Swear to God that you won't torture me!"

For Jesus had said to him, "Come out of this man, you evil spirit!"

Then Jesus asked him, "What is your name?"

"My name is Legion," he replied, "for we are many."

And he begged Jesus again and again not to send them out of the area.

A large herd of pigs was feeding on the nearby hillside.

The demons begged Jesus, "Send us among the pigs; allow us to go into them."

He gave them permission, and the evil spirits came out and went into the pigs. The herd, about two thousand in number, rushed down the steep bank into the lake and were drowned.

Those tending the pigs ran off and reported this in the town and countryside, and the people went out to see what had happened.

When they came to Jesus, they saw the man who had been possessed by the legion of demons, sitting there, dressed and in his right mind; and they were afraid.

Those who had seen it told the people what had happened to the demon-possessed man—and told about the pigs as well.

Then the people began to plead with Jesus to leave their region.

As Jesus was getting into the boat, the man who had been demon-possessed begged to go with him.

Jesus did not let him, but said, "Go home to your family and tell them how much the Lord has done for you, and how he has had mercy on you."

So the man went away and began to tell in the Decapolis how much Jesus had done for him. And all the people were amazed.

MARK 5:1-20, NIV

## INSIGHTS FROM JAMIE BUCKINGHAM

It's possible the man Jesus encountered in the graveyard was a man afraid of wholeness. Yet there was a battle taking place between the mind and the heart—the battle that goes on inside each of us. The heart caused the man to rush to Jesus. The mind caused him to back off and say, "Don't torture me. Leave me alone." Part of him was rushing toward

162

Jesus and the other part was pulling back.

It's the perennial struggle with God. A part of us is saying, "Help me, O Lord," and the other part, clashing, cries, "Don't touch me." Unless settled, such a conflict will make madmen of us all.

There was another instance in the Bible where Jesus had to come back a second time to set a man free. It happened in Bethsaida with a blind man who only received partial sight when Jesus touched him. He returned for a second touch (see Mk 8:22-26). His partial healing was not due to a lack of power in Jesus. Rather, it had to do with the man's will. God never forces us against our will. God waits until our will is ready to be subdued to His will. Then He acts.

The wild man didn't want to be set free. That was evidenced by his statement, "Don't torture me." Any person who genuinely wants to be set free from demon possession can be delivered. In fact, oftentimes just saying, "I want to be set free," brings the release. But when a person does as this man did, there is always a huge struggle.

In this case the demons, hiding behind the man's will, were able to fight back. They were tenacious, yet fearful, for they knew they had met their match.

When Jesus asked, "What is your name?" He was not talking to the man. He was speaking to the devils themselves.

"My name is legion," he replied, "for we are many."

This huge army of demons was no match against the Son of God, whom all God's angels worship (see Heb 1:6). "He became as much superior to the angels as the name He has inherited is superior to theirs" (Heb 1:4).

The demons' greatest fear was banishment from the area where their overlord had assigned them—the area of the

Decapolis. Luke says, "They begged Him repeatedly not to order them to go into the Abyss" (Lk 8:31). The word *Abyss* is capitalized in the original language. It does not refer to the cliff above the sea or the nearby wadis. They were begging, "Don't send us back to hell."

The delivered man, naturally, wanted to go with Jesus; He wanted to become one of His disciples. But Jesus had another plan. The man was to become a witness for Jesus Christ. Earlier, Jesus had told some of His disciples if they would lay down their fishermen's nets and follow Him, He would make them fishers of men. With this man, however, Jesus broke the pattern.

Instead of being a disciple, Jesus wanted Him to be a witness. He was to be a living, walking, unquestionable demonstration of the miracle power of Jesus Christ. Every place this man went, he would be known as a miracle—and no one can argue with a miracle.

—*Miracle Power*

## Questions to Consider
1. What spiritual principle emerges from the story of the demoniac?
2. How can you apply this principle to your life?

## A Prayerful Response
Lord, I believe that in Your name, demons will flee. Amen.

## THE MIRACLE OF FORGIVENESS

### THOUGHT FOR TODAY

When God forgives our sins He infuses His hope into us.

### WISDOM FROM SCRIPTURE

Jesus stepped into a boat, crossed over and came to his own town.

Some men brought to him a paralytic, lying on a mat. When Jesus saw their faith, he said to the paralytic, "Take heart, son; your sins are forgiven."

At this, some of the teachers of the law said to themselves, "This fellow is blaspheming!"

Knowing their thoughts, Jesus said, "Why do you entertain evil thoughts in your hearts?

"Which is easier: to say, 'Your sins are forgiven,' or to say, 'Get up and walk'?

"But so that you may know that the Son of Man has authority on earth to forgive sins...." Then he said to the paralytic, "Get up, take your mat and go home."

And the man got up and went home.

When the crowd saw this, they were filled with awe; and they praised God, who had given such authority to men.

MATTHEW 9:1-8, NIV

### INSIGHTS FROM JAMIE BUCKINGHAM

When Jesus spoke of "their faith," He was not referring to the crowd. He was obviously thinking about the man's four friends. It takes an awful lot of faith to break through the roof of somebody's house and lower a paralytic through the hole into a church service going on down below.

Such faith is still present in the world, still bringing healing. Many can testify to the faith of their parents. Thomas Carlyle once said that still, across the years, there came his mother's voice to him, "Trust in God and do right." The great poet and essayist said his mother's faith strengthened him throughout his life.

When Augustine was living a wild and immoral life, his devout mother came to ask help from a Christian bishop. "It is impossible," the bishop told her, "that the child of so many prayers and tears should perish." Augustine says it was the faith of his godly mother, like the faith of those four friends, that brought him to Jesus.

Sensing the faith in the room, Jesus looked at the paralytic and said simply, "Your sins are forgiven."

Why forgive his sins? What the man needed was a physical overhaul. He was paralyzed. He couldn't walk. It seems that's what most preachers do: They overlook the obvious—the things they can't or won't do anything about—and focus on the spiritual. But remember, the Jews equated all physical suffering with sin. They believed that if a person was suffering, it was the result of sin.

That was the argument Job's "friend," Eliphaz, used. "Who, being innocent, has ever perished? Where were the upright ever destroyed?" he asked Job (see Jb 4:7). He was saying what the old rabbis said much later: "There is no sick man healed of his sickness until all his sins have been forgiven him." That's the reason Jesus began by saying, "Your sins are forgiven."

To the Jews a sick person was a person with whom God was angry.

166

Jesus came to reveal a different God. He said God was a loving heavenly Father. Notice, Jesus did not require anything of the paralytic. He didn't tell him first to confess his sins. He didn't lead him through the "sinner's prayer." He simply looked at him and absolved him of all his sins.

Now we can see why it was imperative for Jesus to forgive the man's sins as a preamble to the miracle about to follow. To have healed the man without forgiving his sins would have been more than the man could take. But once the sin factor was out of the way, he could accept his healing.

"Son," Jesus said to him tenderly, "God is not angry with you. It's OK." To say your sins are forgiven is to say God is not angry. Jesus was doing what He always did—revealing the Father.

All miracles have God's reason behind them. In this case, Jesus said to the man, "Your sins are forgiven," and when He said it, something sparked in his mind. "God is not angry at me. God loves me! There is hope for my life."

Then Jesus said, "Now take up your bed and walk," and suddenly strength went into his body and his back and his legs. But the real miracle happened in his spirit before it happened in his flesh. It happened for the sake of his spirit rather than just for the sake of the flesh.

Why are miracles needed? If we walk as spiritual people, then why miracles? Why don't we walk in health all the time? Why don't we walk in godly protection all the time? Are miracles only for those who are out there living in horrible sin?

No. Miracles are needed because we are sinful people. We live in a sinful world. We are part of a sinful system. We are part of the natural system God has set in order, which has been polluted by humanity. Even though I believe God would have us walk as Adam and Eve, in perfect harmony within nature, we don't do it. Because of evil spirits, because of the Evil One, and because all of us have sinned and come short of the glory of God, we need miracles.

The only way we can exist abundantly on this earth is to walk miracle lives. That's the reason we, as God's people, should expect a miracle every day. We should be living with that expectation. And when we walk into a situation where circumstances say, "The world says this," we should shout, "But God says that; and I'm going to go with God."

—*Miracle Power*

## QUESTIONS TO CONSIDER

1. Are you living with hope? Why, or why not?
2. How might forgiveness of a particular sin renew your hope?

## A PRAYERFUL RESPONSE

Lord, thank You for Your forgiveness and eternal hope. Amen.

## THE GREAT ADVENTURE

### THOUGHT FOR TODAY

God intends for life to be an adventure.

### WISDOM FROM SCRIPTURE

Some time later, Jesus went up to Jerusalem for a feast of the Jews.

Now there is in Jerusalem near the Sheep Gate a pool, which in Aramaic is called Bethesda and which is surrounded by five covered colonnades.

Here a great number of disabled people used to lie—the blind, the lame, the paralyzed.

One who was there had been an invalid for thirty-eight years.

When Jesus saw him lying there and learned that he had been in this condition for a long time, he asked him, "Do you want to get well?"

"Sir," the invalid replied, "I have no one to help me into the pool when the water is stirred. While I am trying to get in, someone else goes down ahead of me."

Then Jesus said to him, "Get up! Pick up your mat and walk."

At once the man was cured; he picked up his mat and walked. The day on which this took place was a Sabbath, and so the Jews said to the man who had been healed, "It is the Sabbath; the law forbids you to carry your mat."

But he replied, "The man who made me well said to me, 'Pick up your mat and walk.' "

So they asked him, "Who is this fellow who told you to

pick it up and walk?"

The man who was healed had no idea who it was, for Jesus had slipped away into the crowd that was there.

Later Jesus found him at the temple and said to him, "See, you are well again. Stop sinning or something worse may happen to you."

The man went away and told the Jews that it was Jesus who had made him well.

JOHN 5:1-15, NIV

## INSIGHTS FROM JAMIE BUCKINGHAM

Life is designed by God to be fun and an adventure. God has placed in each of us a part of His own nature. As the creative part of God is in us (meaning we can't be totally fulfilled unless we are creating), so the adventurous part of God is in us also. We can never be really fulfilled unless we are venturing out—that is, exercising our faith, which is adventure in action. Some people look at circumstances and call them calamities rather than challenges. They do not understand there are no calamities in the life of the believer, only challenges.

This is just as true whether life serves you blindness or a prison cell—all remain great adventures, challenges, opportunities to serve God and exercise great faith in the spirit of adventure.

Does this mean that every blind person should pray for sight? That every prisoner should believe God will throw his cell open as He did for Peter and later for Paul and Silas? No, but it does mean that when circumstances visit us with blindness, incarceration or paralysis, we must answer the question: "Do I want to be healed, do I want to see, do I want to be set free?" If you do, there are certain things God will require of you—and many are not willing to pay the price.

Life is designed to be an adventure. Jesus knew that, of course, since He was the architect who was with the Creator when life was formed. Thus, when He came to earth and saw this wretched old man at the Pool of Bethesda, the first question He asked was, "Is the spirit of adventure still alive, or have you given up hope?"

The man Jesus questioned had been trapped by life's circumstances. For thirty-eight years he had been lying there, looking for a cure. Many adults are like that. Their entire adult life has been spent in the doctor's office. They go to the doctor three times a week. They are more familiar with the doctor's office than they are with their own home. They know where all the magazines are. Any time they feel a twitch of pain they contact their insurance company or some government agency. They don't want to be well. Sickness is their way of life. To change it would deprive them of their happiness, their identity.

So many are like this man. They may not be paralyzed in body, but their brain has stopped hoping, their heart has stopped believing. The adventurous spirit has been crushed by life's calamities. Locked in a cell, disabled by disease, deserted by loved ones, ostracized by society, doomed to live alone when everything in them cries out for companionship—they simply give up.

When pushed into that kind of situation, God would have us say, "I'm going to do something with this. By God's strength, I'll make it work!"

Jesus' question did not deal just with illness. It dealt with wholeness. "Do you want to be made whole?" Do you want life now, in the present? Do you want the spirit of adventure restored to you?

Despite the man's seemingly poor answer, Jesus saw something in him the man didn't even see in himself. He looked deep inside of the man and saw thirty-eight years of being crushed by disease and pain. He didn't rebuke the man for his superstition. Rather, He took what little faith the man had—the faith that if he could ever reach the water he'd be healed—and blessed that faith. The man wanted to be healed, even though he thought he never could be since he had no one to help him. So Jesus, looking deep into the man's heart, spoke the word of healing.

That is all that's ever necessary for healing—whether it is healing for a broken heart or a crippled body. All that's needed is a word from God.

God will heal anyone on the basis of His mercy. But there is great evidence that He prefers to heal on the basis of inheritance. God wants to use us to heal others. God wants His miracles to come through us. That way He is sure to get the glory, for everyone knows people do not have the power to heal cripples by a spoken word. When it happens, it is obvious God has inhabited that person, and the word spoken in faith is actually the word of God.

—*Miracle Power*

## QUESTIONS TO CONSIDER
1. What great adventure do you want for your life?
2. Do you feel free to ask God for it? Explain.

## A PRAYERFUL RESPONSE
Lord, fill my life with Your adventures. Amen.

# DAY 36

## Our Sovereign God

### Thought for the Day

Miracles express God's goodness, providence and faithfulness.

### Wisdom From Scripture

As he went along, he saw a man blind from birth.

His disciples asked him, "Rabbi, who sinned, this man or his parents, that he was born blind?"

"Neither this man nor his parents sinned," said Jesus, "but this happened so that the work of God might be displayed in his life.

"As long as it is day, we must do the work of him who sent me. Night is coming, when no one can work.

"While I am in the world, I am the light of the world."

Having said this, he spit on the ground, made some mud with the saliva, and put it on the man's eyes.

"Go," he told him, "wash in the Pool of Siloam" (this word means Sent). So the man went and washed, and came home seeing.

His neighbors and those who had formerly seen him begging asked, "Isn't this the same man who used to sit and beg?"

Some claimed that he was. Others said, "No, he only looks like him." But he himself insisted, "I am the man."

"How then were your eyes opened?" they demanded.

He replied, "The man they call Jesus made some mud and put it on my eyes. He told me to go to Siloam and wash. So I went and washed, and then I could see."

JOHN 9:1-11, NIV

## INSIGHTS FROM JAMIE BUCKINGHAM

A miracle, basically, is the intervention of a higher law over a lower law. God has, in the creation of the earth, set in motion certain physical laws that govern the universe. There are laws of psychology and human behavior, laws of health, laws of physics, laws of engineering—many different kinds of laws.

But there are other laws that are invisible to us—visible only to God—which control the kingdom of heaven. A miracle is basically the imposition of the laws of the kingdom of heaven over the laws of this world.

What activates these higher laws remains a mystery. There are certain factors that often set them in motion. Prayer, for instance.

Prayer is not necessarily a group of people getting together and fasting and waiting on God, then asking God to meet their need. Nor is it somebody standing up in an auditorium and praying vocally. Praying has many different kinds of connotations. In basic form prayer is, as James Montgomery said, "the soul's sincere desire." God listens to the heart. So prayer seems to be one of the things that keys off miracles.

Faith is another element that seems to be important in laying the foundation for miracles to happen. Jesus loved to ask people if they believed He could perform a miracle. For instance, when two blind men came to Him crying, "Have mercy on us, Son of David," Jesus turned and asked, "Do you believe that I am able to do this?"

"Yes, Lord," they replied.

He then touched their eyes and they were able to see. His explanation: "According to your faith will it be done to you" (see Mt 9:27-31).

Yet we find miracles happening to people who don't believe, just as we find miracles happening to folks who don't pray. Therefore, at the heart of every miracle is the providence and goodness and the faithfulness of God.

Faith, human desire, radical circumstances, the taking of spiritual authority ... all of these can play a part. Yet in the long run we are still subject to the sovereignty of God, and it is God alone who makes the final decision—sometimes totally apart from even the prerequisites set in Scripture.

But there are certain factors that put certain miracles into effect at certain times. It is up to us to discern these, for it is obvious that God intends for miracles to be as much in evidence today as they were when Jesus was here in the flesh, and He wants them to occur through us. He wants us to be people who are not just governed by the laws of this universe but by the kingdom of God.

The Bible tells us we need to walk in both realms. We must obey the laws here. We can't get out on the highway and drive 120 miles an hour just because our speedometer says we can and believe that God will miraculously take us through the heavy traffic. He wants to work in balance with the laws of this world as well as with the higher laws of the kingdom.

There may be a time, for instance, when we need to drive above the posted speed limit for the sake of saving someone's life. There may be a time when we need to pick up a poisonous snake, or are bitten by one accidentally. God does not give us license to pick up snakes to test our faith, any more than He gives us license to drive recklessly.

But we need to remember He is a God of miracles; and if He has given us a commission—as He gave Paul when

He told him to go to Rome—then no poisonous snake will thwart us as we carry it out.

*—Miracle Power*

## QUESTIONS TO CONSIDER
1. When asking for a miracle, how might you know when to obey natural laws?
2. How can you know when to ask God to override nature's laws?

## A PRAYERFUL RESPONSE
Lord, help me to discern Your sovereign will about miracles. Amen.

## HOPE FOR THE HOPELESS

### THOUGHT FOR TODAY

To give God glory, we need to testify concerning His miracles.

### WISDOM FROM SCRIPTURE

When he came down from the mountainside, large crowds followed him.

A man with leprosy came and knelt before him and said, "Lord, if you are willing, you can make me clean."

Jesus reached out his hand and touched the man. "I am willing," he said. "Be clean!" Immediately he was cured of his leprosy.

Then Jesus said to him, "See that you don't tell anyone. But go, show yourself to the priest and offer the gift Moses commanded, as a testimony to them."

MATTHEW 8:1-4, NIV

While Jesus was in one of the towns, a man came along who was covered with leprosy. When he saw Jesus, he fell with his face to the ground and begged him, "Lord, if you are willing, you can make me clean."

Jesus reached out his hand and touched the man. "I am willing," he said. "Be clean!" And immediately the leprosy left him.

Then Jesus ordered him, "Don't tell anyone, but go, show yourself to the priest and offer the sacrifices that Moses commanded for your cleansing, as a testimony to them."

Yet the news about him spread all the more, so that crowds of people came to hear him and to be healed of their sicknesses.

LUKE 5:12-15, NIV

## INSIGHTS FROM JAMIE BUCKINGHAM

There were proper channels for the confirmation of a healing in the biblical period. Jesus did not want to deliberately antagonize the priests in the temple. For the most part, they were doing the best they could to serve God with their limited vision and understanding. Instead, He realized this would be a wonderful opportunity to glorify God as a God of miracles among the religious leaders.

Even though there was a complicated ceremony outlined in Leviticus 14 to declare a leper clean, it was seldom used except in the case of skin disease, for leprosy was considered hopeless. There was no known cure.

Jesus had pointed this out at the beginning of His public ministry when He stood in the synagogue at Nazareth and read from the prophet Isaiah, proclaiming Himself the Messiah. In His explanation to the people He said, "And there were many in Israel with leprosy in the time of Elisha the prophet, yet not one of them was cleansed—only Naaman the Syrian" (Lk 4:27).

The reference is to a remarkable story in 2 Kings 5. Naaman, the king of Syria, had leprosy. Humbling himself, he came to the Jewish prophet Elisha, asking for help. Elisha told him to dip himself in the Jordan River seven times. Naaman did and was healed. It was another evidence of God's miraculous healing power.

When Jesus reminded the Jews in Nazareth of this, and in so doing let them know that He had the same power as

Elisha, they tried to kill Him. No mortal, they knew, had the power to cure leprosy. Only God could do that.

Jesus wanted the priests in the temple to know God was curing leprosy. He warned the man to be careful not to tell anyone else, for He did not want the people to try to force Him to become a military Messiah. Instead, Jesus encouraged the man to use the proper and accepted (although never used) procedure for ceremonial cleansing.

The ceremony of restoration from "unclean" to "clean" was complicated, but filled with beautiful symbolism. The man had to present himself to the priest for a physical examination, bringing with him two birds. One of the birds was killed over running water. The living bird was then dipped in the blood of the dead bird, along with cedar, scarlet and hyssop and allowed to fly free. The man then washed himself and shaved, changed his clothes and seven days after presented himself again for examination of his skin. This time he sacrificed two male lambs without blemish and one ewe lamb and a mixture of flour and oil. Pronouncing the man clean, the priest would touch him on the tip of the right ear, the right thumb and the right big toe with blood and oil. He was then given a certificate, declaring him restored.

Such a ceremony would doubtlessly draw a great deal of attention. So despite Jesus' admonition, "Don't tell anyone," the word was going to get out.

Healings today should be confirmed by proper authorities—either spiritual authorities or medical people. Testimony is needed that the God of miracles is still touching people and healing them.

*—Miracle Power*

## Questions to Consider

1. Have you told others of God's miraculous power?
2. How can you testify to "the proper authorities" about God's miracles?

## A Prayerful Response

Lord, I will tell others about Your miraculous work in me. Amen.

# DAY 38

## ENOUGH FOR EVERYONE

### THOUGHT FOR TODAY
God can multiply the resources in your life.

### WISDOM FROM SCRIPTURE
Some time after this, Jesus crossed to the far shore of the Sea of Galilee (that is, the Sea of Tiberias), and a great crowd of people followed him because they saw the miraculous signs he had performed on the sick.

Then Jesus went up on a mountainside and sat down with his disciples.

The Jewish Passover Feast was near.

When Jesus looked up and saw a great crowd coming toward him, he said to Philip, "Where shall we buy bread for these people to eat?"

He asked this only to test him, for he already had in mind what he was going to do.

Philip answered him, "Eight months' wages would not buy enough bread for each one to have a bite!"

Another of his disciples, Andrew, Simon Peter's brother, spoke up, "Here is a boy with five small barley loaves and two small fish, but how far will they go among so many?"

Jesus said, "Have the people sit down." There was plenty of grass in that place, and the men sat down, about five thousand of them.

Jesus then took the loaves, gave thanks, and distributed to those who were seated as much as they wanted. He did the same with the fish.

When they had all had enough to eat, he said to his disciples, "Gather the pieces that are left over. Let nothing be wasted."

So they gathered them and filled twelve baskets with the pieces of the five barley loaves left over by those who had eaten.

After the people saw the miraculous sign that Jesus did, they began to say, "Surely this is the Prophet who is to come into the world."

JOHN 6:1-14, NIV

## INSIGHTS FROM JAMIE BUCKINGHAM

What happened here? I have heard all kinds of explanations. Nobody really knows. How did the miracle of multiplication take place? Did it take place in the blessing—as Jesus blessed the loaves, did they just get bigger and bigger? Did it take place in the distribution—as the disciples took the five loaves and went out to distribute them did more bread simply appear in their hands? Did it take place in the eating? When did the miracle story take place?

Even though this is the only miracle story recounted by all four biographers, not a single word is said about the actual method of the miracle. In fact, it seems to be a deliberate omission, as if the Holy Spirit forbade the writers to recount it—a phenomena that occurs with all the other miracles as well. Some things are hidden, not just to keep us from trying to imitate them, or to prevent us from making a sacred formula out of them, but because they are incomprehensible. They remain, and ever will be, mysteries.

The real impact of this passage is not in the mechanics of the miracle. The real impact is in what caused it to take place to start with—a couple of hearts turned toward God. Jesus believed, of course. (He already knew what was going to happen.) Then there was a little kid who brought his meal and said, "Take mine." He gave everything. And there was a disciple who said, "It's not very much, but maybe we can do a little bit with it."

God looked upon all those things, and the miracle of multiplication took place. Enough for everyone.

One twentieth-century Bible commentary has an interesting theory about the feeding of the five thousand. He suggests that the miracle was not in the multiplication of the food but in the spirit of unselfishness that swept through the crowd when they saw the little boy offer up his meager lunch.

These pilgrims on their way to Jerusalem for the feast of Passover would have certainly had food with them, stashed away in their own baskets. But they were stingy, afraid to share for fear they would use up all their food before the end of the trip. But when they saw the generosity of a small boy, it pricked their hearts. When Jesus blessed the five loaves and started passing them out, they reached into their baskets and brought out their own loaves—sharing them also.

This is a very beautiful story. Maybe it happened that way. God is capable, of course, of making stingy people generous. But I suspect had it really happened that way, at least one of the four biographers would have mentioned it. Instead, all leave the impression it was a genuine miracle of multiplication. It was a miracle of provision.

We are dealing with a God of miracles who loves to intervene in people's lives, who loves to change the course of physical action. Many times all He is waiting for is somebody who will say, "Here's my lunch, Jesus, do with it what You will."

Unlike people, Jesus did not want applause. He fed the people because He loved them. He performed His miracle to show practical-minded Philip and the other disciples that God is not limited to engineering principles, that He doesn't always follow the rules of the financial planner, and that He sometimes blesses foolish people. The same God who turned water into wine when the host miscalculated, also fed five thousand people who foolishly got trapped away from home without any food.

Jesus exhibits this principle here. "I did it because I loved them, that was all," Jesus said to His disciples when the miraculous meal was over. "Now, let's get out of here before they try to make Me king."

God loves those who help people and then don't hang around to get any credit.

—*Miracle Power*

## QUESTIONS TO CONSIDER
1. Do you need a miracle of multiplication in your life? If so, what would it be?
2. How can you express your faith for this miracle?

## A PRAYERFUL RESPONSE
Lord, multiply Your goodness in my life. Amen.

## Power Over Evil

### Thought for Today
Drawing near to God, we need not fear evil.

### Wisdom From Scripture
When they came to the other disciples, they saw a large crowd around them and the teachers of the law arguing with them.

As soon as all the people saw Jesus, they were overwhelmed with wonder and ran to greet him.

"What are you arguing with them about?" he asked.

A man in the crowd answered, "Teacher, I brought you my son, who is possessed by a spirit that has robbed him of speech.

"Whenever it seizes him, it throws him to the ground. He foams at the mouth, gnashes his teeth and becomes rigid. I asked your disciples to drive out the spirit, but they could not."

"O unbelieving generation," Jesus replied, "how long shall I stay with you? How long shall I put up with you? Bring the boy to me."

So they brought him. When the spirit saw Jesus, it immediately threw the boy into a convulsion. He fell to the ground and rolled around, foaming at the mouth.

Jesus asked the boy's father, "How long has he been like this?"

"From childhood," he answered. "It has often thrown him into fire or water to kill him. But if you can do anything, take pity on us and help us."

"'If you can'?" said Jesus. "Everything is possible for him who believes."

Immediately the boy's father exclaimed, "I do believe; help me overcome my unbelief!"

When Jesus saw that a crowd was running to the scene, he rebuked the evil spirit. "You deaf and mute spirit," he said, "I command you, come out of him and never enter him again."

The spirit shrieked, convulsed him violently and came out. The boy looked so much like a corpse that many said, "He's dead."

But Jesus took him by the hand and lifted him to his feet, and he stood up.

After Jesus had gone indoors, his disciples asked him privately, "Why couldn't we drive it out?"

He replied, "This kind can come out only by prayer. "

MARK 9:14-29, NIV

## INSIGHTS FROM JAMIE BUCKINGHAM

Do you see what Jesus did? He walked down into the valley, grabbed hold of this man's spirit and put him up on the Mount of Transfiguration, where they had all been just before. Then He said, "Even though you live in the valley, your spirit can live on the mountaintop." The man grabbed hold of that and said, "Hallelujah! I don't ever want to go back down there again."

It was then Jesus rebuked the evil spirit.

He called the spirit by name. He knew what it was. Matthew suggests the boy had epilepsy. Epilepsy, of course, is a legitimate disease that is caused by problems with electrical impulses in the brain. That's not to say all epilepsy is caused by demons. But anytime you see a situation where there is a weakness in the human body, you will find Satan attacking that particular weakness by sending his demons to try to take over. In the case of this boy, they had succeeded.

Does this mean demons are responsible for every sickness, every impossible situation? Of course not. Most of the people Jesus healed were not afflicted by demons. However, the wise Christian knows he should be on the lookout for demonic presence—even when ministering to children. That's awesome, to think that a child can be possessed by a demon. However, we find at least two other occurrences in the Scriptures where they brought children to Jesus who were demon-possessed. In each of these instances, Jesus cast out the demons.

Here He does the same thing. He speaks to the demon, and there is a physical manifestation. Demons seldom leave a person peacefully. They hate to leave, and often tear and rip a person as they are forced to leave under the authority of Jesus. But leave they must when a believer takes authority over them. The Bible says, "The word [of God] is very nigh unto thee, in thy mouth" (Dt 30:14). The name of Jesus in the mouth of a believer is the most powerful force in the world.

It was a total and complete deliverance. In this case the boy's illness was caused by a demon. By removing the demon from the situation, the illness cured itself.

Jesus says this kind of demon can come out only through prayer, or prayer and fasting. What was He talking about? Jesus didn't stop and pray or fast. He didn't say, "Wait here, I'll be back in three days after I've fasted and prayed." He just spoke the word and the demon left.

But, in fact, Jesus had just come down from the mountain

where He had been praying and fasting. He had not been praying and fasting for this little boy. But Jesus lived a "fasted life." He was not only prepared to give up food, He was prepared to give up His very life. He lived a cross-life, a life of constant sacrifice. No demon can withstand that kind of life. No wonder when He spoke, the demon had to leave.

So Jesus said to His disciples, "You don't live close enough to God. If you lived close enough to God you would be equipped with power." God gives us gifts, but they are useless unless we use them for Him.

There is a profound lesson here: What we do in private, in our relationship with God, is more important than what we do in public. If we do things in private in our relationship with God, He will use us in public ministry elsewhere. All He requires is that we remain close to Him.

*—Miracle Power*

## Questions to Consider
1. In the presence of evil, how can you draw near to God?
2. How can you prepare in private for public ministry?

## A Prayerful Response
Lord, prepare me in private for Your public ministry. Amen.

## POWER OVER DEATH

### THOUGHT FOR TODAY

God wants to resurrect the dead places in our souls.

### WISDOM FROM SCRIPTURE

When Mary reached the place where Jesus was and saw him, she fell at his feet and said, "Lord, if you had been here, my brother would not have died."

When Jesus saw her weeping, and the Jews who had come along with her also weeping, he was deeply moved in spirit and troubled.

"Where have you laid him?" he asked.

"Come and see, Lord," they replied.

Jesus wept.

Then the Jews said, "See how he loved him!"

But some of them said, "Could not he who opened the eyes of the blind man have kept this man from dying?"

Jesus, once more deeply moved, came to the tomb. It was a cave with a stone laid across the entrance.

"Take away the stone," he said.

"But, Lord," said Martha, the sister of the dead man, "by this time there is a bad odor, for he has been there four days."

Then Jesus said, "Did I not tell you that if you believed, you would see the glory of God?"

So they took away the stone. Then Jesus looked up and said, "Father, I thank you that you have heard me.

"I knew that you always hear me, but I said this for the

benefit of the people standing here, that they may believe that you sent me."

When he had said this, Jesus called in a loud voice, "Lazarus, come out!"

The dead man came out, his hands and feet wrapped with strips of linen, and a cloth around his face. Jesus said to them, "Take off the grave clothes and let him go."

JOHN 11:32-44, NIV

## INSIGHTS FROM JAMIE BUCKINGHAM

It is not enough to have life. We need to be set free. So many of us have experienced life but have never tasted the freedom of the Holy Spirit. We're still bound to our grave clothes. We need to ask ourselves the question: "Am I alive or dead? If I am alive, am I still bound in the old grave wrappings of sin and tradition? Do I need someone to help me, or do I prefer to remain in the shadows?"

Jesus sought only the glory of God. When Elijah had his encounter with the prophets of Baal on Mount Carmel he prayed, "Answer me, O Lord, answer me, so these people will know that you, O Lord, are God ..." (1 Kgs 18:37). Jesus never did anything to draw attention to Himself. His single purpose on earth was to glorify His Father in heaven.

How different people are, even people of God, who seem to draw attention to themselves. So much of what we do is an attempt, by our own power, to raise ourselves in the eyes of others. What we wear, how (and where) we live, our transportation, our jewelry, our cosmetics—all frequently are designed to bring glory to self.

It was by God, and for God, that Jesus acted. Perhaps we would have more miracles in our lives if we, too, ceased to act by our own strength and for our own self and began acting only in the power of God and for His glory.

One day I decided I wanted to find out what the world looked like as a small child. I got down on the floor with my three-year-old grandson and walked around on my knees. Everything was different from that perspective. I thought, *What would it be like if I had to walk through life less than three feet tall?* I would never be able to see facial expressions. It would be impossible to understand the world of adults.

Perhaps that's what Jesus was weeping about. He so wanted His friends to understand God, but they were earthbound. It took a miracle to bring revelation—much as if God had picked us up in His arms and said, "Come up here for a minute and see what the kingdom is really like. Up here you understand what authority you really have—even authority over death."

With a word, time was turned around. It was just a few miles from there, in the valley of Ajalon, that one thousand years before, Joshua had pointed to the sun and the moon and commanded them to stand still. Everything had stopped so that God's people could get their job done. Here Jesus pointed at time and said, "Go back." And Lazarus came forth from the grave.

What became of Lazarus after his resurrection? There is no record, but the ancient legends say he always seemed to be a bit melancholy—as if he had experienced something wonderful that no one else could fully understand. For as wonderful as it is to be called back from the dead, it is far more wonderful to receive a resurrection into life eternal.

—*Miracle Power*

## QUESTIONS TO CONSIDER

1. How has death touched your life?
2. How can you bring Christ's resurrection power to death's presence?

## A PRAYERFUL RESPONSE

Lord, I celebrate that Your resurrection conquered death. Amen.

# Books by Jamie Buckingham

*A Way Through the Wilderness*
*Bible People Like Me*
*Coming Alive*
*Coping with Criticism*
*Daughter of Destiny*
*Jamie Buckingham on the Miracles of Jesus*
*Jesus World*
*Into the Glory*
*Let's Talk about Life*
*Look Out World—I'm Me!*
*Miracle Power*
*Parables*
*Power for Living*
*Risky Living*
*Some Gall*
*Summer of Miracles*
*The Nazarene*
*The Last Word*
*The Parables of Jesus*
*The Truth Will Set You Free,*
*but First It Will Make You Miserable*
*Where Eagles Soar*
*Your New Look*

# Books Co-Written With Jamie Buckingham

*10,000 Miles for a Miracle* (Kathryn Kuhlman)

*A Glimpse into Glory* (Kathryn Kuhlman)

*Ben Israel* (Art Katz)

*Call to Discipleship* (Juan Carlos Ortiz)

*Capt. Levrier Believes in Miracles* (Kathryn Kuhlman)

*From Harper Valley to the Mountaintop* (Jeannie C. Riley)

*God Can Do It Again* (Kathryn Kuhlman)

*How Big Is Our God* (Kathryn Kuhlman)

*Let's Begin Again* (Father Sherwood)

*Medicine to Miracles* (Kathryn Kuhlman)

*Mission: An American Congressman's Voyage into Space*
(Bill Nelson)

*Never Too Late* (Kathryn Kuhlman)

*Nothing Is Impossible with God* (Kathryn Kuhlman)

*O Happy Day* (The Happy Goodman Family)

*Run Baby Run* (Nicky Cruz)

*Shout It from the Housetops* (Pat Robertson)

*Standing Tall* (Kathryn Kuhlman)

*The Coming Food Crisis* (Frank Ford)

*The End of Youngblood Johnson* (Aaron Johnson)

*The Lonely Now* (Nicky Cruz)

*Tramp for the Lord* (Corrie ten Boom)

*Twilight to Dawn* (Kathryn Kuhlman)

# ABOUT THE COMPILER

With the *Life Messages* devotional series, Judith Couchman hopes you'll be encouraged and enlightened by people who have shared their spiritual journeys through the printed word.

Judith owns Judith & Company, a writing and editing business. She has also served as the creator and founding editor-in-chief of *Clarity* magazine, managing editor of *Christian Life,* editor of *Sunday Digest,* director of communications for The Navigators and director of new product development for NavPress.

Besides speaking to women's and professional groups, Judith has authored and compiled twenty-three books and many magazine articles. In addition, she has received numerous awards for her work in secondary education, religious publishing and corporate communications.

She lives in Colorado.